Free Video — Free Video

Essential Test Tips Video from Trivium Test Prep

Dear Customer,

Thank you for purchasing from Trivium Test Prep! We're honored to help you prepare for your exam.

To show our appreciation, we're offering a **FREE** *Essential Test Tips* **Video by Trivium Test Prep.*** Our video includes 35 test preparation strategies that will make you successful on your big exam. All we ask is that you email us your feedback and describe your experience with our product. Amazing, awful, or just so-so: we want to hear what you have to say!

To receive your **FREE** *Essential Test Tips* **Video,** please email us at 5star@triviumtestprep.com. Include "Free 5 Star" in the subject line and the following information in your email:

1. The title of the product you purchased.
2. Your rating from 1 – 5 (with 5 being the best).
3. Your feedback about the product, including how our materials helped you meet your goals and ways in which we can improve our products.
4. Your full name and shipping address so we can send your **FREE** *Essential Test Tips* **Video.**

If you have any questions or concerns please feel free to contact us directly at 5star@triviumtestprep.com.

Thank you!

– Trivium Test Prep Team

*To get access to the free video please email us at 5star@triviumtestprep.com, and please follow the instructions above.

CNA STUDY GUIDE:

2022-2023: Review Manual with Practice Test Prep Questions and Detailed Answers for the NNAAP Certified Nursing Assistant Exam

E. M. Falgout

Copyright © 2022 by Ascencia Test Prep

ISBN-13: 9781637989005

ALL RIGHTS RESERVED. By purchase of this book, you have been licensed one copy for personal use only. No part of this work may be reproduced, redistributed, or used in any form or by any means without prior written permission of the publisher and copyright owner. Ascencia Test Prep; Trivium Test Prep; Accepted, Inc.; and Cirrus Test Prep are all imprints of Trivium Test Prep, LLC.

The National Council of State Boards of Nursing, Inc. was not involved in the creation or production of this product, is not in any way affiliated with Ascencia Test Prep, and does not sponsor or endorse this product. All test names (and their acronyms) are trademarks of their respective owners. This study guide is for general information only and does not claim endorsement by any third party.

Image(s) used under license from Shutterstock.com

Table of Contents

Online Resources i
Introduction iii

1 Activities of Daily Living 1
- Hygiene 1
- Dressing and Grooming 6
- Nutrition and Hydration 9
- Elimination 12
- Patient Comfort and Safety 16
- Fall Prevention 16
- Lifting, Transferring, and Positioning Patients 17
- Range of Motion Exercises 20
- Answer Key 22

2 Basic Nursing Skills 23
- The Physical Exam 23
- Positioning Patients 23
- Vital Signs 25
- Specimen Collection and Testing 30
- Wounds 32
- Restraints 33
- Answer Key 34

3 Safety and Infection Control 35
- Infection Control 35
- Emergency Response 41
- Fire and Electrical Safety 46
- Answer Key 48

4 Psychosocial Care Skills 49
- Emotional, Spiritual, and Cultural Needs 49
- Mental Health Needs 50
- Answer Key 52

5 Role of the Nurse Aide 53
- Communication 53
- Client Rights 54
- Legal and Ethical Behavior 56
- Members of the Health Care Team .. 57
- Answer Key 59

6 Practice Test 61
- Answer Key 69

Online Resources

To help you fully prepare for your CNA exam, Ascencia includes online resources with the purchase of this study guide.

PRACTICE TEST

In addition to the practice test included in this book, we also offer an online exam. Since many exams today are computer based, getting to practice your test-taking skills on the computer is a great way to prepare.

FLASH CARDS

A convenient supplement to this study guide, Ascencia's flash cards enable you to review important terms easily on your computer or smartphone.

CHEAT SHEETS

Review the core skills you need to master the exam with easy-to-read Cheat Sheets.

FROM STRESS TO SUCCESS

Watch "From Stress to Success," a brief but insightful YouTube video that offers the tips, tricks, and secrets experts use to score higher on the exam.

REVIEWS

Leave a review, send us helpful feedback, or sign up for Ascencia's promotions—including free books!

Access these materials at: **https://www.ascenciatestprep.com/cna-online-resources**.

INTRODUCTION

Congratulations on choosing to take the Certified Nurse Assistant/Aide (CNA) exam! Passing the CNA exam is an important step forward in your health care career, and we're here to help you feel prepared on exam day.

The certification process for nurse assistants/aides varies from state to state. The information in this introduction will cover the details of the National Nurse Aide Assessment Program (NNAAP) exam, which is used in the following states and territories:

- Alabama
- Alaska
- California
- Colorado
- District of Columbia
- Georgia
- Maryland
- Minnesota
- Mississippi
- New Hampshire
- North Carolina
- Pennsylvania
- Rhode Island
- South Carolina
- Texas
- Virginia
- Virgin Islands
- Washington

If your state or territory doesn't use the NNAAP exam, don't worry! The concepts and practice questions in this book can still help you prepare for your state's exam. Check with your state's Nurse Aide Registry to find out how to become certified in your state.

The Certification Process

The National Nurse Aide Assessment Program (NNAAP) exam includes a written exam and practical skills evaluation. To qualify for the exams, candidates must have completed a state-approved nurse assistant/aide training course within the previous two years. Some states will also allow candidates with other training (e.g., licensed nurse coursework) to qualify for certification. The exam is given at Pearson VUE testing centers, and applications for the exam are completed on the Pearson VUE website. You can visit the NNAAP website at https://www.ncsbn.org/nnaap-and-mace.htm to find the application for your state.

The Written/Oral Exam

The written exam consists of 70 multiple-choice questions. Ten of these questions are unscored: they are included on the exam so the test makers can try out new questions. You will have two hours to complete the exam.

Candidates who have difficulty reading English may take the multiple-choice exam in an oral format. Some states also offer a Spanish language version of the oral exam. The candidate will be able to listen to the questions and will then mark the correct answer in the test booklet. The oral form of the test includes the same number of questions as the written form.

The written/oral exam covers three content areas that test the candidate's knowledge of terms, concepts, and skills relevant to being a nurse assistant/aide.

CNA Exam Content

Content Area	Detailed Content	Number of Scored Questions
I. Physical Care Skills	Activities of Daily Living • hygiene • dressing and grooming • nutrition and hydration • elimination • rest/sleep/comfort	9
	Basic Nursing Skills • infection control • safety/emergency • therapeutic and technical procedures • data collection and reporting	23
	Restorative Skills • prevention • self care/independence	5
II. Psychosocial Care Skills	Emotional and Mental Health Needs	6
	Spiritual and Cultural Needs	2
III. Role of the Nurse Aide	Communication	4
	Client Rights	4
	Legal and Ethical Behavior	2
	Member of the Health Care Team	5
Total		**60**

The Skills Evaluation

The skills evaluation is a practical, hands-on exam that requires candidates to perform nurse assistant/aide skills. The skills will be demonstrated on a simulated patient using real equipment. A Nurse Assistant Evaluator will compare your performance to the required steps listed in the NNAAP Skills List.

The NNAAP list includes 22 tested skills. You will be asked to perform **FIVE** of these skills. Some states have a skill that is always included on the exam (e.g., handwashing), but this varies by state.

NNAAP SKILLS LIST FOR SKILLS EVALUATION

- Skill 1: Hand Hygiene (Hand Washing)
- Skill 2: Applies One Knee-High Elastic Stocking
- Skill 3: Assists to Ambulate Using Transfer Belt
- Skill 4: Assists with Use of Bedpan
- Skill 5: Cleans Upper or Lower Denture
- Skill 6: Counts and Records Radial Pulse
- Skill 7: Counts and Records Respirations
- Skill 8: Donning and Removing PPE (Gown and Gloves)
- Skill 9: Dresses Client with Affected (Weak) Right Arm
- Skill 10: Feeds Client Who Cannot Feed Self
- Skill 11: Gives Modified Bed Bath (Face and One Arm, Hand and Underarm)
- Skill 12*: Measures and Records Electronic Blood Pressure
- Skill 13: Measures and Records Urinary Output
- Skill 14: Measures and Records Weight of Ambulatory Client
- Skill 15: Performs Modified Passive Range of Motion (PROM) for One Knee and One Ankle
- Skill 16: Performs Modified Passive Range of Motion (PROM) for One Shoulder
- Skill 17: Positions on Side
- Skill 18: Provides Catheter Care for Female
- Skill 19: Provides Foot Care on One Foot
- Skill 20: Provides Mouth Care
- Skill 21: Provides Perineal Care (Peri-Care) for Female
- Skill 22: Transfers from Bed to Wheelchair Using Transfer Belt
- Skill 23: Measures and Records Manual Blood Pressure

Skill 12: Measures and Records Electronic Blood Pressure is no longer tested.

In this study guide, we have included all the skills in special boxes alongside the relevant study content. These boxes provide simplified, step-by-step instructions for each skill. Steps in bold are **critical element steps**: if these steps are not completed correctly, you will fail that skill. For the complete list of skills, visit the Pearson VUE website.

Exam Administration

To register for the exam, you must first apply through the Pearson VUE website (https://home.pearsonvue.com/test-taker). You will be asked to submit the necessary documents to prove that you meet the eligibility requirements. Once the appropriate state agency has approved your application, you will be scheduled to take the exam.

The exam is offered at Pearson VUE testing centers. You will have three months from the acceptance of your application to take the exam. If you do not take the exam within the three-month window, you will have to resubmit your application.

Plan to arrive at least 30 minutes before the exam to complete biometric screening. You will need two forms of government-issued ID. Be prepared to be photographed and have your palm scanned. Your primary ID must be government issued, include a recent photograph and signature, and match the name under which you registered to take the test. If you do not have proper ID, you will not be allowed to take the test.

You will not be allowed to bring study material or electronic devices, including phones, programmable calculators, or smart watches, into the testing room. The testing site will provide lockers for valuables.

Exam Results

How you receive your results will depend on the state you test in. Some states deliver results on the same day as the test. In other states, you will receive your results through your Pearson VUE account after several days.

If you fail either the written/oral exam or the skills evaluation, you will be able to retake the exam. In most states, you will have three chances to take the exam. If you fail three times, you will have to retake a nursing assistant/aide training course.

Using This Book

This book is divided into two sections. In the content area review, you will find a summary of the knowledge and skills included in the exam content outline. Throughout the chapter you'll also see Quick Review Questions that will help reinforce important concepts and skills.

The book also includes two full-length practice tests (one in the book and one online) with answer rationales. You can use these tests to gauge your readiness for the test and determine which content areas you may need to review more thoroughly.

Ascencia Test Prep

With health care fields such as nursing, pharmacy, emergency care, and physical therapy becoming the fastest-growing industries in the United States, individuals looking to enter the health care industry or rise in their field need high-quality, reliable resources. Ascencia Test Prep's study guides and test preparation materials are developed by credentialed industry professionals with years of experience in their respective fields. Ascencia recognizes that health care professionals nurture bodies and spirits, and save lives. Ascencia Test Prep's mission is to help health care workers grow.

ONE: ACTIVITIES of DAILY LIVING

Hygiene

ORAL CARE

Oral care prevents tooth decay and odors and promotes comfort. Many different medical conditions can cause oral problems. However, every patient, regardless of diagnosis, requires oral care. Equipment for providing oral care includes a towel, facecloth, paper towels, gloves, toothpaste, toothbrush, toothette (swab), floss, cup of water, kidney basin, and mouthwash.

> **Skills Evaluation: Provide Mouth Care**
> 1. Wash hands and put on gloves.
> 2. Place patient in upright position (75 – 90 degrees).
> 3. Place towel across patient's chest.
> 4. Moisten toothbrush in cup of water and apply paste.
> 5. **Gently brush entire mouth, including teeth and tongue.**
> 6. Give patient a sip of water to rinse mouth while holding basin to their chin.
> 7. Wipe patient's mouth.
> 8. Dispose of linens and rinse equipment.
> 9. Remove gloves and wash hands.

HELPFUL HINT
For the skills evaluation:
- Start the skill by explaining the procedure to the patient and closing the curtain for privacy.
- End each skill by disposing of gloves and washing hands.

Flossing should be done after brushing the patient's teeth. When preparing to floss a patient's teeth, first ensure that flossing is not contraindicated. To start, break off a piece of floss, and move it gently up and down between teeth. Start at the back of the right side of the mouth and work around to the left side.

Denture care includes the cleaning and proper storage of patient dentures. The nurse aide may need to remove the dentures from the patient's mouth by grasping them lightly with a piece of gauze. Once clean, place dentures in a cup labeled with the patient's name and other necessary information (e.g., room number).

HELPFUL HINT
Always watch for signs of choking when providing mouth care.

Skills Evaluation: Clean Upper or Lower Denture

1. Wash hands and put on gloves.
2. Line sink with a towel.
3. Rinse dentures under lukewarm water.
4. Brush dentures with soft brush and denture paste.
5. Rinse dentures and denture cup.
6. Place dentures in denture cup half-filled with water or solution.
7. Dispose of towel and rinse toothbrush.
8. Remove gloves and wash hands.

HELPFUL HINT
Never use hot water or regular toothpaste on dentures.

HELPFUL HINT
Avoid triggering the gag reflex when swabbing the tongue and roof of mouth.

When providing oral care for unconscious patients, treat the patient as if they were conscious (i.e., identify yourself and explain the task). If not contraindicated, raise the bed to 30 degrees and position the patient close to the side of the bed before starting.

Once the patient is positioned, place a towel under the patient's head and a basin beneath their chin. Apply water-soluble lubricant to the patient's lips, and gently separate the patient's jaw with a padded tongue depressor. (Never force the teeth apart.) Wet a toothette with the prescribed solution or mouthwash. Squeeze out excess solution and thoroughly swab the mouth from top to bottom.

When cleaning is finished, use chlorhexidine mouthwash or water to rinse the toothettes. Change toothette as needed.

QUICK REVIEW QUESTION

1. After cleaning dentures, the nurse aide should place the clean dentures:
   A) on a clean, dry towel next to the sink.
   B) in a cup of water on the patient's bedside.
   C) back in the patient's mouth.
   D) in the appropriate trash receptacle.

BATHING

Bathing can help a patient feel better, improve circulation, prevent odors and infection, and provide an opportunity to spot an injury. Follow the physician's orders and the patient's preferences regarding when and how often the patient should bathe and what cleansers to use.

Equipment includes gloves, at least two towels, five to six washcloths, bath blankets, bed linen to change the patient's bedding, a wash basin with warm water, skin cleanser, skin lotion or skin barrier cream, and clean clothing.

Bed baths are given to patients who cannot bathe in a tub or shower. Start with the face, then move to the arms, chest, legs, and feet. Place a towel under each limb before washing, and pat each area dry before moving on. To finish, turn patient on their side and wash from the neck down to the buttocks.

Privacy is a priority when giving bed baths: always cover areas not being washed. Use new washcloths when moving to a new area, and change water when it is soapy, dirty, or cold. After the bath is complete, ensure that the areas between the toes, under the breasts, and inside skin folds are dry before dressing the patient.

Skills Evaluation: Give Modified Bed Bath (Face and One Arm, Hand and Underarm)

1. Wash hands.
2. Remove patient's gown and dispose of it properly. (Keep the patient's chest and lower body covered with a blanket.)
3. Test water temperature for safety and comfort.
4. Put on gloves.
5. Wash face with a wet facecloth with no soap. Begin with inner aspect of eyes and expand to the rest of the face. Use a new spot on the facecloth each time.
6. Dry face.
7. Uncover arm to be washed and place towel underneath.
8. Apply soap to washcloth and gently wash fingers, hand, arm, and underarm. Dry washed area.
9. Dress patient in a clean gown.
10. Clean, store, or dispose of linen and supplies appropriately, observing clean technique.

Patients who are able to leave their bed may take **tub baths**. The nurse aide may provide various levels of assistance. They may simply be present and available for help when asked, or they may need to assist the patient with bathing. Some guidelines for tub baths are given below.

- Always clean the tub before bathing a patient.
- Ensure side rails, call light, and other safety equipment are in working order before bringing patient to the tub.
- Ask the patient to void before starting the bath.
- Remove hearing aids and glasses before helping patient into bathtub.
- Monitor patient for weakness or dizziness.
- Tub baths should be no longer than 20 minutes.
- Check water temperature for safety and comfort.
- Never fill the tub higher than waist deep.
- Keep soap bar out of the water when not washing. Do not use oils in a tub or a shower.
- Use a nonskid mat for patient to stand on when they exit the tub.
- Use the same order as the bed bath, starting with the eyes and ending with the perineal area. Wet and shampoo hair if requested.

The main responsibility of the nurse aide when assisting with **showers** is to maintain the patient's safety. There is a greater risk of dizziness or falls if a patient stands to bathe.

Patients should use a bench or chair if they are a fall risk. There is also a risk for chills if the patient is not under the stream of water, especially with a handheld shower nozzle.

Guidelines for showers are similar to those for tub baths. Provide the requested amount of bathing assistance, and monitor for safety risks.

Perineal care should be done when bathing and whenever the patient has urine or feces on them. It prevents infection, promotes comfort, and prevents odors. Some general guidelines for perineal care are given below.

- For females, separate the labia with one hand, and wipe one side, the other side, then the middle with the other hand.
- For males, retract the foreskin if the patient is uncircumcised. Start at the meatus and wipe downward in a circular motion. Replace the foreskin when done.
- Always use a new area of the washcloth and a single stroke from top to bottom.
- Change washcloths when soiled. Do not reuse dirty washcloths or place them in the water basin.

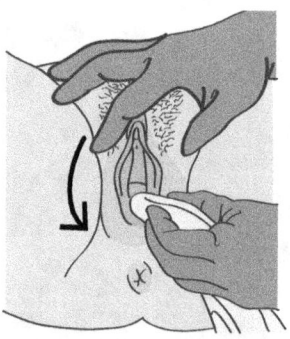

Figure 1.1. Direction of Movement for Perineal Cleaning

> ### Skills Evaluation: Provide Perineal Care (Peri-Care) for Female
> 1. Test water temperature in basin for safety and comfort.
> 2. Put on gloves.
> 3. Place pad under buttocks and perineal area.
> 4. Expose the patient's body from hips to knees.
> 5. **Using soapy washcloth, wash perineal area, wiping front to back, using new area of washcloth each time.**
> 6. **With new wet washcloth, rinse the perineal area using the same method.**
> 7. Dry perineal area with towel using the front-to-back method.
> 8. Roll patient to their side in the lateral or Sims position, and repeat procedure for rectal area.
> 9. Reposition patient in semi-Fowler's position and ensure comfort.
> 10. Clean, store, or dispose of linens and supplies appropriately, observing clean technique.

QUICK REVIEW QUESTION

2. During a tub bath, the nurse aide should FIRST wash the client's:
   A) hands.
   B) feet.
   C) eyes.
   D) perineal area.

BEDMAKING

Bedmaking promotes comfort and prevents skin breakdown and infections. Bed linen should be changed immediately when wet or dirty. If not visibly wet or soiled, linens should be changed once a day in acute care and once a week in long-term care or in a patient's home. Bedmaking is usually done when the patient takes a bath or shower.

Beds are made differently based on the needs of the client.

- A **closed bed** is made for patients who are out of bed during the day.
- An **open bed** is ready for the patient to use.
- A **surgical bed** is prepared for patients being transferred from a stretcher.

HELPFUL HINT
Never shake linens or put linens on the floor.

When making any bed, the first step is to collect the linens in the order that they will be put on the bed. Carry linens away from body, and put clean linens down on clean and dry surfaces. Collected linens may include:

- bottom sheet
- top sheet
- blanket
- pillowcase for each pillow
- mattress pad, drawsheet, waterproof under-pad, or bed protector (as needed)

To make an **unoccupied bed**, start by removing dirty linens from the bed. Bag linens if they are contaminated and dispose of them properly. Used linens should never come in contact with the floor or furniture.

Make the bed starting with the bottom sheet (or mattress pad if requested). If using a flat sheet as a bottom sheet, use **mitered corners**. If a drawsheet or waterproof pad is being used, place it in position in the center of the bed. Place the top sheet and blanket on the bed, then tuck the top linens under the bottom of the bed using a mitered corner. Do not tuck in the sides of the top sheet or blanket.

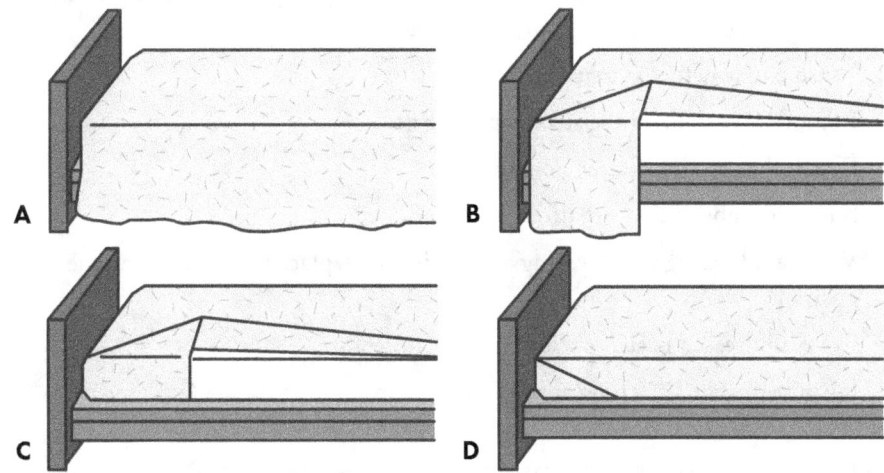

Figure 1.2. Mitered Corners

Then, put the pillow in the pillowcase and place on bed. When making a closed bed, the top linens are left unfolded (either over or under the pillow). When making an open bed, the top linens should be fan folded to the end of the bed.

To make an **occupied bed**, start by covering the patient with a bath blanket and removing the top sheet. Next, roll patient on their side and fan fold used linens toward

HELPFUL HINT
When making an occupied bed, change gloves after touching dirty linens and before touching clean linens.

the client. Place a clean bottom sheet and drawsheet (as needed) on the empty half of the bed and fan fold it toward the client.

The client can then be turned on their other side. Remove the dirty linens, and finish putting the bottom sheet and drawsheet on the bed. Shift patient to the supine position, and put on the top sheet and blanket. Tuck top linens under the bottom of the bed using a **toe pleat**.

To make a surgical bed, put on the bottom sheet and top sheet. Next, fan fold the top sheet vertically to one side of the bed. Put the pillow in the pillowcase and place it to the side of the bed on a clean surface.

QUICK REVIEW QUESTION

3. To remove the top sheet from an occupied bed, the nurse aide SHOULD:
    A) drape the patient with a bath blanket and remove the top sheet from underneath.
    B) roll the patient to their side facing away and fold the sheet toward the far rail.
    C) position the patient supine and fold the sheet toward the foot of the bed.
    D) assist the patient to a sitting position next to the bed and remove the top sheet.

Dressing and Grooming
DRESSING

Undressing and dressing patients should be done with concern for the dignity and independence of the patient. Invite patients to participate to the extent of their abilities, and allow them to choose their own clothes when appropriate. Other guidelines for undressing and dressing patients are given below.

- Wash hands before starting.
- Remove garments on the stronger side first.
- Put clothes on the weaker side first.
- Support limbs as they are lifted or moved.
- When undressing and dressing a client in a bed, place them in the supine position.
- Cover undressed patients with a bath blanket.
- Dispose of soiled clothing appropriately.

> **Skills Evaluation: Apply One Knee-High Elastic Stocking**
> 1. Position patient in the supine position.
> 2. Turn stocking inside out to the heel.
> 3. Place over patient's toes, and pull over patient's foot and leg.
> 4. **Ensure heel of stocking is over heel, toe opening is over toes, and there are no twists or wrinkles.**
> 5. Wash hands.

Skills Evaluation: Dress Client with Affected (Weak) Right Arm

1. Ask patient what shirt they would like to wear.
2. Carefully remove gown from the left arm and then from the right arm while avoiding exposure of patient's chest.
3. Dispose of gown in dirty linen container.
4. Carefully pull shirt over patient's head, and pull on the right sleeve and then the left sleeve.
5. Straighten shirt and reposition patient.
6. Wash hands.

QUICK REVIEW QUESTION

4. Garments should be removed starting with the:
   A) weaker side.
   B) stronger side.
   C) right side.
   D) left side.

HAIR CARE

Brushing hair increases blood flow to the scalp and keeps hair from becoming matted. Provide hair care when it is needed or requested. Some general guidelines for brushing hair are given below.

- Wear gloves if there are scalp sores or a large amount of matting or dirt.
- Be sure there are no broken or sharp bristles or teeth in the brush/comb.
- Place a towel behind the patient's head or on their shoulders to catch falling hair.
- Comb curly or coarse hair starting from the nape and move upward, fluffing hair.
- Comb straight hair from the top of the head. Smooth hair downward.
- For hair tangles, hold hair with one hand above the tangle and comb out the tangle. Avoid pulling at the patient's scalp.

Shampooing hair may be done daily or a few times a month. Many long-term care residents have their hair washed on their bath day or in the hair salon. The tub or shower typically has a handheld spray that facilitates shampooing. For bedbound patients, some facilities have an inflatable basin to wash their hair in bed.

When shampooing, focus on patient safety by keeping water and soap out of the patient's eyes. (A washcloth may be used to cover their eyes.) Also make sure not to scrape or damage the scalp when massaging the shampoo into the hair. Remove items that may be damaged by water (e.g., hearing aids) before starting.

Safety is also an important focus when **shaving** patients. Safety razors may be used for most patients. However, patients at high risk for bleeding or skin injury (e.g., those with diabetes or bleeding disorders) may require the use of an electric razor. If bleeding occurs, apply pressure and report per facility policies.

HELPFUL HINT
Always report any sores, hair loss, or the presence of nits or lice.

Always moisten the area to be shaved before starting, and use shaving cream. Hold skin taut, and shave in the direction of hair growth except when shaving the legs or using a rotary shaver.

QUICK REVIEW QUESTION

5. A nurse aide is brushing a client's hair and notices sores on the scalp. The nurse aide SHOULD:
   A) offer to shampoo the client's hair.
   B) tell the client to report the sores to their doctor.
   C) clean and bandage the sores.
   D) report the sores to the nurse.

NAIL AND FOOT CARE

Trimming nails prevents infections, odors, torn nails, and lacerations. For patients with conditions that impede healing (e.g., diabetes), a small injury in their foot can lead to serious complications. For this reason, most facilities do not allow nurse aides to trim nails. If the nurse aide is asked to trim nails, they should use caution if the patient has diabetes, circulation problems, an ingrown nail, or are on medications that cause bleeding. General guidelines for nail trimming are given below.

- Soak nails before trimming (5 to 10 minutes for fingernails; 15 to 20 minutes for toenails).
- Clean under nails with an orange stick. Clean the orange stick with a towel after each nail.
- Gently push back patient's cuticles with the orange stick.
- Clip nails straight across and file any roughness with an emery board.
- Apply lotion after hands or feet are clean and dry.
- Report to the nurse any injuries or signs of infection such as blisters or ingrown toenails.

HELPFUL HINT
Never leave water or lotion between a patient's toes.

Skills Evaluation: Provide Foot Care on One Foot

1. Check water temperature for safety and comfort.
2. Lay down protective barrier, and place basin where patient can put their foot in it.
3. Put on gloves.
4. Place patient's foot in the water.
5. Lift foot and wash with soapy washcloth.
6. Rinse foot with water.
7. Dry foot, ensuring areas between toes are dry.
8. Apply lotion to the foot (all areas except between toes).
9. Clean, store, or dispose of supplies using clean technique.

QUICK REVIEW QUESTION

6. A nurse aide is trimming a patient's fingernails and cuts too deep, causing the client to bleed. The nurse aide SHOULD:

A) clean and bandage the wound.

B) leave the wound alone and get the nurse.

C) apply pressure to the wound and alert the nurse.

D) place the client's hand back in the water basin until the bleeding stops.

Nutrition and Hydration

NUTRITION BASICS

Food provides **nutrients**: the molecules that provide energy and the chemical building blocks the body needs to function. There are five main groups of nutrients.

- **Carbohydrates** are sugars that provide easily accessible energy for cells.
- **Fats** are molecules that store energy for later use.
- **Proteins** perform a wide range of functions in the body, including providing structural support in cells and tissues.
- **Vitamins** are molecules the body needs in small amounts to function but cannot make on its own.
- **Minerals** are elements (e.g., calcium) that the body requires to function.

People must eat a balance of different foods to meet their nutritional needs. The United States Department of Agriculture (USDA) has created dietary guidelines called **MyPlate** to help people eat appropriate amounts of fruits, vegetables, grains, protein, and dairy foods.

- **Grains** are foods made from wheat, rice, and other cereal crops. They are high in carbohydrates.
- **Fruits** are the seed-bearing parts of plants. They provide essential vitamins and minerals and are low fat. However, they may contain high amounts of sugar.
- **Vegetables** are the leaves, stalks, and roots of plants. They provide essential vitamins and minerals and are usually low in fat and sugar.
- **Dairy** products are made from milk. They contain calcium and vitamin D, which are essential for bone health.
- **Protein** can come from animal sources (e.g., beef) or plant sources (e.g., tofu).

Special diets are defined by their texture or the type of food they contain. Clients may require special diets to manage allergies, physical limitations, metabolic disorders, or medication interaction. They may also follow special diets for cultural or religious reasons.

- diabetic diet: strictly regulated carbohydrate consumption
- low-sodium diet: low in salt
- cardiac diet: restricted fat and salt

HELPFUL HINT

Calories are a measure of the energy in food. Fats are the most calorie-dense nutrient (9 calories per gram).

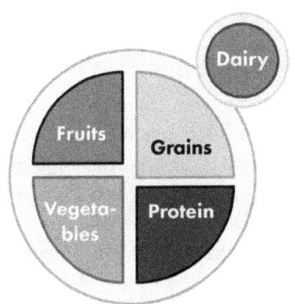

Figure 1.3. MyPlate Serving Suggestions

HELPFUL HINT

Dysphagia is difficulty swallowing. Clients with dysphagia may require a special diet (e.g., mechanically soft) to reduce the risk of choking.

- clear liquid diet: liquids only, including water, clear broth, and popsicles
- full liquid diet: foods that become a liquid at body temperature such as ice cream or cooked cereal
- mechanical soft diet: semi-solid, easily digestible food like scrambled eggs and shredded meats
- residue-free diet: low in indigestible food like fiber and seeds
- high-fiber diet: high in fiber such as fruits and whole grains
- bland diet: low-fiber foods without strong spices such as white toast or cottage cheese
- high-calorie diet: intake of 3,000 or 4,000 calories a day
- limited-calorie diet: restricted calories to promote weight loss
- vegetarian diet: no meat
- vegan diet: no meat, dairy, or other animal products
- kosher diet: food prepared according to Jewish dietary laws
- halal diet: food prepared according to Islamic dietary laws

QUICK REVIEW QUESTION

7. What type of diet might be ordered to help a patient with constipation?
   A) high fiber
   B) clear liquid
   C) vegetarian
   D) low sodium

HYDRATION BASICS

Hydration is the balance of fluids in the body. Adequate fluid intake prevents conditions related to dehydration, including constipation, urinary tract infections, dizziness, and heart problems.

Fluid balance is often assessed by measuring a client's **intake and output (I&O)**. Input is all the fluids the client consumes; output is all the fluid excreted from the body. Intake and output are measured in milliliters (mL). Common conversion amounts for intake include:

- 1 teaspoon = 5 mL
- 1 tablespoon = 15 mL
- 1 ounce = 30 mL
- 1 cup = 240 mL
- 1 pint = 500 mL

HELPFUL HINT

Patients who have dysphagia will drink thickened liquids to prevent choking. Some liquids come ready-made in the proper consistency, while others must be prepared by the nurse aide.

Some patients have special orders affecting their intake of fluids. **NPO** is Latin for *nil per os* and means "nothing by mouth." Patients on NPO cannot eat or drink. **Encourage fluids** means that something to drink should be offered as often as possible and be kept within reach. Patients listed as **restrict fluids** are allowed a limited amount of fluids determined by the doctor.

QUICK REVIEW QUESTION

8. A patient who is NPO asks the nurse aide for a lunch tray. The nurse aide SHOULD:
   A) tell the patient they cannot eat any food and alert the nurse to the patient's request.
   B) offer the patient a glass of water instead.
   C) leave a lunch tray but tell the patient to talk to their nurse before eating.
   D) offer a snack but tell the patient they cannot tell the nurse they ate.

ASSISTING WITH MEALS

When assisting patients with meals, the nurse aide should focus on patient safety and independence. Many patients who require assistance to eat may have difficulties with chewing or swallowing, so the nurse aide should continually monitor for choking. The nurse aide should also follow protocols to ensure patients on special diets eat the appropriate food.

Patients require varying levels of assistance with eating. The nurse aide should encourage independence by having the patient participate as much as possible. Patients may be able to select which foods they want, eat some foods by hand, or hold certain utensils or cups.

Other general guidelines for feeding are given below.

- Match patient's name to name on food tray and check allergies.
- Sit facing the patient to watch for signs of choking.
- Report signs of difficulty swallowing to the nurse.
- Review the contents of the tray with the patient, and ask what they would prefer to eat first. Defer to the patient's preferences.
- Use a spoon to prevent injuries. Bites of food should be ½ of the spoon or smaller.
- Ensure mouth is empty before offering another bite of food. Do not rush the patient.
- For patients with impaired vision, describe what is on their plate and where it is using a clock pattern.
- Encourage patient to drink fluids by offering fluids throughout the meal.
- Never give a patient a cup with hot liquid in it.
- Wipe patient's face with a napkin when needed.
- At the end of the meal, verify patient is full and document the percentage eaten.

Skills Evaluation: Feed Client Who Cannot Feed Self

1. Match patient's name with name on tray.
2. **Place patient in upright position (high Fowler's).**
3. Place tray where patient can see it easily.
4. Clean patient's hands.
5. Sit facing the patient.
6. Identify food on the tray, and ask what the patient wants to eat first.

7. Using a spoon, offer patient a bite of each food. Identify each food when offered.
8. Offer beverages at least once during the meal.
9. Ask patient if they are ready for another bite of food before giving it.
10. When done, clean patient's hands and mouth.
11. Wash hands.

QUICK REVIEW QUESTION

9. When feeding a client, the nurse aide SHOULD offer fluids:
    A) only at the beginning of the meal.
    B) only at the end of the meal.
    C) regularly throughout the meal.
    D) after each bite of food.

Elimination

ASSISTING WITH ELIMINATION

A **bedpan** is used for elimination when a patient cannot get out of bed. The bedpan is positioned under the patient when they need to urinate or have a bowel movement. Most patients will use a regular bedpan, but patients with hip or spinal injuries may use a **fracture pan**.

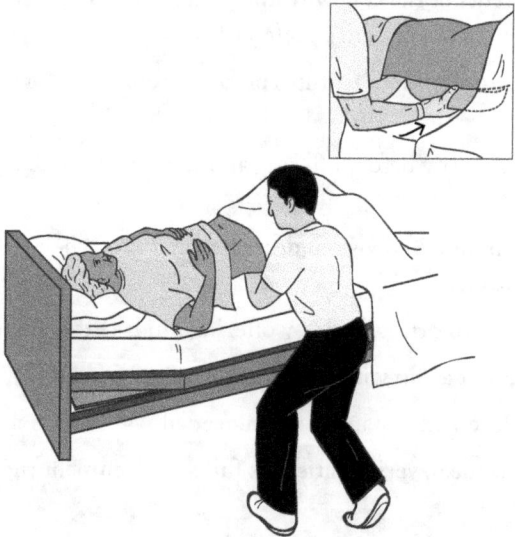

Figure 1.4. Positioning Bedpan

Skills Evaluation: Assist with Use of Bedpan

1. Lower head of bed.
2. Put on gloves.
3. Cover patient with a blanket.

4. Place protective barrier and bedpan under patient's buttocks.
5. Remove gloves and wash hands.
6. Raise head of bed.
7. Place toilet tissue, call light, and hand wipes within reach.
8. Ask patient to use hand wipes and press call light when done.
9. When patient presses call light, wash hands and put on gloves.
10. Lower head of bed.
11. Ask patient to lift buttocks or roll patient to their side and remove bedpan.
12. Empty bedpan into toilet. Rinse bedpan and pour rinse into toilet.
13. Place bedpan in appropriate dirty supply area.
14. Remove gloves and wash hands.

Men use **urinals** to void urine in bed. The nurse aide may need to assist the patient by bringing the urinal to the patient, assisting them into a sitting position, or positioning the urinal for the patient. When the patient is done, the nurse aide should note the output and empty the urinal into the toilet. Follow appropriate protocol to ensure urine does not contaminate clean surfaces.

If the patient can stand and transfer, they may use a **commode**. The commode should be positioned next to and facing the foot of the bed like a wheelchair. The nurse aide should make sure the wheels on the commode are locked before the patient leaves the bed. The patient can be assisted into and off the commode similar to a chair.

Incontinence products include adult diapers, liners, and protective pads (disposable or reusable) with an absorbent layer on one side and a moisture barrier on the other. Incontinence is a major cause of skin irritation, and most patients require a moisture barrier cream when using incontinence products.

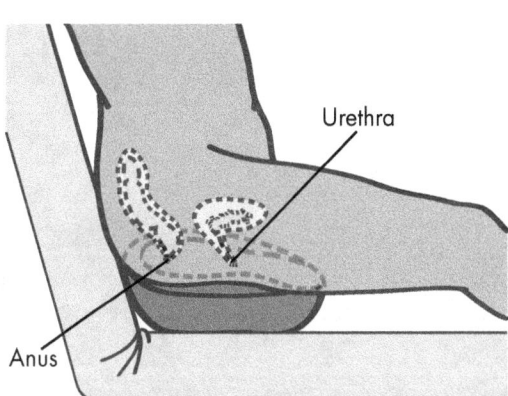

Figure 1.5. Bedpan Position During Elimination

QUICK REVIEW QUESTION

10. Moisture barrier cream should be applied to a patient's perineal area:
    A) before a clean incontinence product is applied.
    B) before they use a commode.
    C) after they use bedpan for a bowel movement.
    D) after a condom catheter has been secured.

URINARY CATHETERS

Indwelling catheters (or Foley catheters) are inserted through the urethra into the bladder to continuously drain urine. The urine is collected in a **drainage bag**, which may be attached to the patient's leg or bed.

Drainage bags must be emptied regularly. The amount of urine in the drainage bag may need to be recorded as part of I&O. This may be done through a gauge on the drainage bag or by draining urine from the bag into a graduate.

HELPFUL HINT
Urinary catheter drainage bags should always be kept below the level of the bladder to allow for drainage.

HELPFUL HINT
Signs of UTI include reduced output, blood in urine, and pain during urination. Report signs of a UTI to the nurse immediately.

Indwelling catheters create a high risk of **urinary tract infection (UTI)**, so the nurse aide must be meticulous when cleaning catheters and changing drainage bags. The connection between the catheter and drainage tube should be sterile. When reconnecting the drainage bag, the ends must be wiped with antiseptic. When changing a bag, do not touch the sterile cap or plug that connects the catheter to the drainage bag.

Catheter care includes cleaning the exposed portion of the catheter from the meatus. Clean at least 4 inches of the tube. Catheter care may also include perineal cleaning.

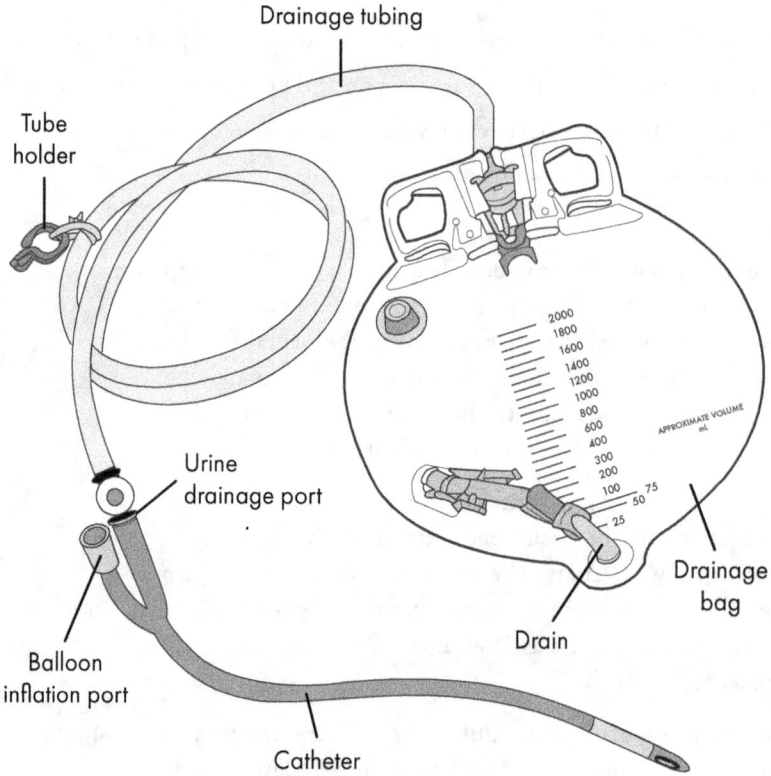

Figure 1.6. Indwelling Catheter

Skills Evaluation: Provide Catheter Care for Female

1. Check temperature of water for safety and comfort.
2. Put on gloves.
3. Place protective barrier under buttocks.
4. Expose patient between hips and knees.
5. Stabilize the catheter with one hand being careful not to pull it.
6. Use a soapy washcloth and wipe downward, away from the meatus, at least 4 inches. Use a clean section of the washcloth for each wipe.

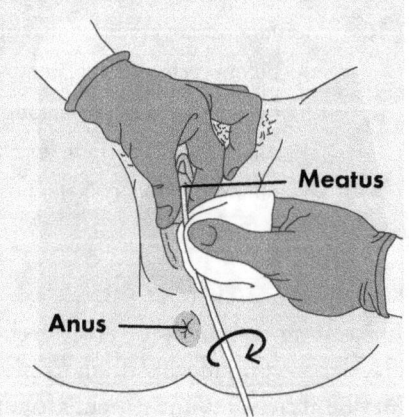

Figure 1.7. Cleaning a Female Catheter

7. Use the same procedure to rinse and then dry the catheter.
8. Cover and reposition the patient.
9. Clean, store, and dispose of supplies appropriately.

Condom catheters are secured over the penis with elastic tape to catch urine. They should be changed daily as part of perineal care. Use only the tape provided by the manufacturer to secure the catheter—other types of adhesive may restrict blood flow to the penis. To apply a condom catheter, hold the penis firmly while unrolling the condom and leave a space of one inch at the tip of the condom.

QUICK REVIEW QUESTION

11. When reconnecting the drainage tube to an indwelling catheter, the nurse aide SHOULD:
    A) clean the inside of the drainage tube with soapy water.
    B) secure the drainage tube to the catheter with elastic tape.
    C) hang the drainage bag above the level of the bladder.
    D) wipe the end of the drainage tube with an antiseptic wipe.

BOWEL ELIMINATION

Fecal impaction occurs when a patient has had long-term constipation. Notify the nurse if the patient has no stools, loose stools, abdominal pain, or distension. The nurse may do a digital rectal exam to check for an impaction. The doctor may order laxatives, suppositories, or an enema to encourage bowel elimination. The nurse may remove the impaction, or they may ask the nurse aide to remove it.

To remove the impaction, place the patient in Sims position. Insert a lubricated, gloved finger into the rectum, massage around the hardened feces, and gently pull a small amount out.

Removing impacted feces in the rectum can be dangerous. It may stimulate the vagus nerve, cause a perforation, or cause bleeding. Stop the procedure and report to the nurse if the patient bleeds, has an irregular pulse, loses consciousness, or experiences pain.

Enemas are liquids that stimulate movement of the bowels. The type of fluid used is determined by the physician. (Nurses must administer enemas containing medications.) Enemas are administered with the patient in Sims position. The lubricated tip of the enema tube is inserted into the rectum, and the fluid is slowly drained into the rectum. After an enema, the nurse aide should be prepared to provide the patient with a bedpan or commode, or to move them to the toilet so they can defecate.

Ostomies are openings that allow drainage from organs (e.g., bladder, intestine) outside the body. The opening on the skin's surface is called a **stoma**. Ostomies typically empty into an **ostomy bag** that can be opened at the bottom to be drained into the toilet. The ostomy bag is changed every 2 to 7 days.

HELPFUL HINT
Suppositories are medications absorbed in the rectum. Because they are medications, suppositories are inserted by nurses. However, the nurse aide may be asked to assist.

QUICK REVIEW QUESTION

12. After a patient receives an enema, the nurse aide should be prepared to:
    A) keep the patient NPO for 8 hours.
    B) place the patient in high Fowler's position.
    C) provide the patient with a meal tray.
    D) assist the patient with bowel elimination.

Patient Comfort and Safety

The nurse aide has a duty to help patients feel safe and comfortable. When performing tasks with patients, the nurse aide should always prioritize these needs. Patients may also tell the nurse aide when they are uncomfortable or have unmet needs. The nurse aide should meet these requests when able and should report complaints of pain or inadequate care to the nurse.

Some other guidelines for promoting patient safety and comfort are below.

- Defer to the patient regarding any personal preferences or rituals.
- Position the patient properly.
- Keep the patient's clothes and bed linens clean and wrinkle-free.
- Adjust the room temperature and lighting levels per the patient's request.
- Organize patient care tasks so the patient's sleep is uninterrupted.
- Provide a calm, dark environment for sleep.
- Use a gentle touch and a soft voice when providing care.
- Avoid sudden movements and loud noises.
- Facilitate patient visits with supportive family.

QUICK REVIEW QUESTION

13. A client who is having his vital signs checked every four hours complains to the nurse aide that he cannot get enough sleep. How should the nurse aide respond?
    A) "Everyone has to have their vital signs taken at night."
    B) "I'm sorry you are not getting enough sleep. I will speak with the nurse about changing your schedule."
    C) "Sleep is very important. I will stop taking your vital signs at night and instead come in the morning."
    D) "I'm sorry, but I can't change your schedule. Maybe you can take a nap during the day."

Fall Prevention

Falls are the most common cause of injury in medical care. Fall risk is increased by many different factors, including increased age and certain medical conditions. Follow general fall risk guidelines for all patients, regardless of risk.

- Keep floor clear of clutter.
- Ensure patient's basic needs are met (e.g., they are hydrated, they can eliminate as needed).

- Place call light and equipment (e.g., eyeglasses, canes) within the patient's reach.
- Respond to call lights and alarms promptly.
- Use side rails and wheel locks on beds and stretchers.
- Keep the patient's bed in the appropriate position.
- Use the necessary staff and equipment for providing care.
- Ensure patients wear non-slip footwear.
- Do a safety check of the patient's room after visitors leave.

HELPFUL HINT
Never use one patient's equipment with another patient.

QUICK REVIEW QUESTION

14. All of the following are responsibilities of the nurse aide related to fall prevention EXCEPT:
- A) picking up clutter from the room floor.
- B) putting up side rails after transferring a patient to the bed.
- C) monitoring the patient's sedation level.
- D) providing nonslip footwear for the patient.

Lifting, Transferring, and Positioning Patients

The nurse aide needs to know how to safely move and position patients in the bed and how to **transfer** patients to and from the bed. Always follow general safety guidelines for lifting and transferring patients, regardless of the patient's functional status.

- Know the procedure, equipment, and number of staff needed for the move/transfer before starting.

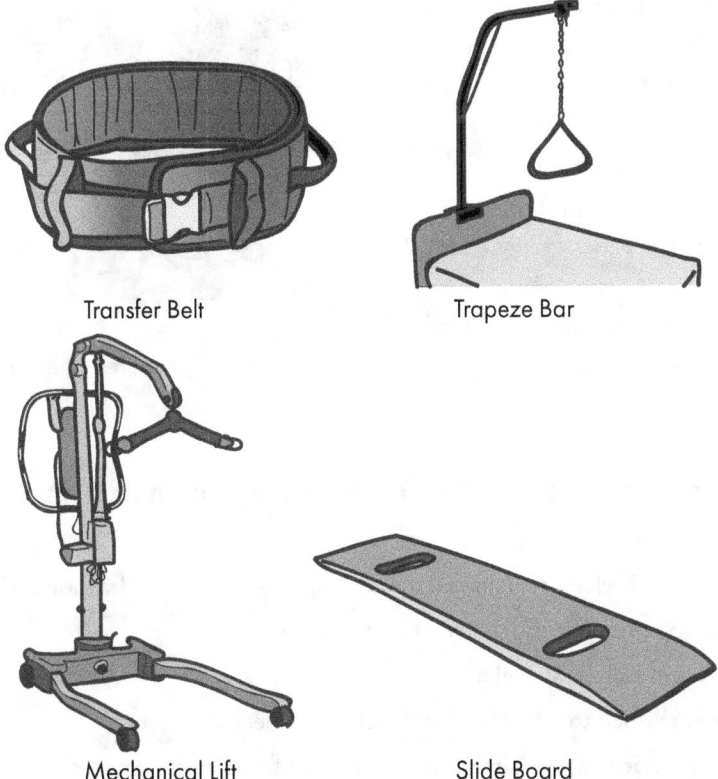

Figure 1.8. Transfer Assist Devices

ACTIVITIES OF DAILY LIVING 17

HELPFUL HINT
Always use the lift procedure and equipment outlined in the care plan. If the appropriate equipment is not available, alert the nurse.

- Promote patient participation when appropriate. It provides the patient with a sense of autonomy and minimizes the strain on the caregiver's body.
- Always bend at knees (not at waist) when lifting.
- Stop the move/transfer and return patient to original position if they report pain.
- Use a predetermined signal (e.g., on the count of three) to start the lift.
- Keep the patient's body in a comfortable and correctly aligned position when moving/transferring.
- Always lock the wheels on beds, stretchers, and wheelchairs when moving/transferring patients.
- Use appropriate position devices to promote comfort and prevent injury (e.g., pressure ulcers).

Skills Evaluation: Assist to Ambulate Using Transfer Belt

1. **Ensure client is wearing non-skid footwear.**
2. Lower bed to a safe level and lock wheels.
3. **Assist patient into a sitting position with feet flat on the floor.**
4. Apply transfer belt securely over clothing.
5. Explain procedure to patient and agree on a signal to begin standing.
6. Stand facing patient (knee to knee or toe to toe) with an upward grasp on the transfer belt at the patient's sides.
7. Direct patient to stand using an agreed-upon signal.
8. Assist patient to stand.
9. Walk behind and slightly to the side of the patient for at least 10 feet.
10. Assist patient back into bed and remove the belt.
11. Wash hands.

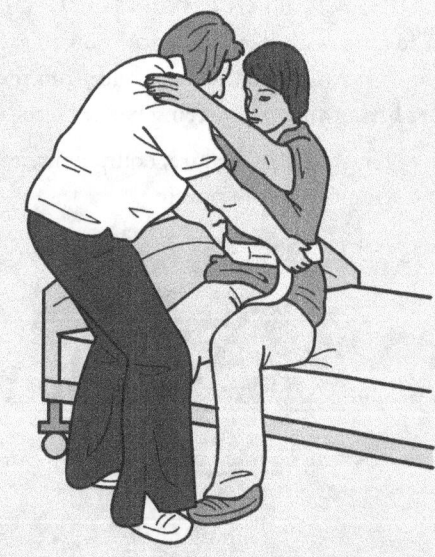

Figure 1.9. Transfer Belt Position

Skills Evaluation: Transfer from Bed to Wheelchair Using Transfer Belt

1. Position wheelchair alongside the bed facing the head or the foot of the bed.
2. Fold up or remove the footrests on the wheelchair.
3. **Lock wheelchair wheels.**
4. Lower the bed to a safe level and lock bed wheels.
5. **Assist patient into a sitting position with feet flat on the floor.**

6. Ensure patient is wearing non-slip shoes.
7. Fasten transfer belt at patient's waist over their clothes.
8. Explain the procedure to the patient and agree on a signal to begin standing.
9. Stand facing patient (knee to knee or toe to toe) with an upward grasp on the transfer belt at the patient's sides.
10. Direct patient to stand using an agreed-upon signal.
11. Help client position themselves in front of the wheelchair with the back of their legs against the wheelchair.
12. Help patient sit down with hips against the back of the wheelchair.
13. Remove transfer belt.
14. Reapply footrests and position patient.
15. Wash hands.

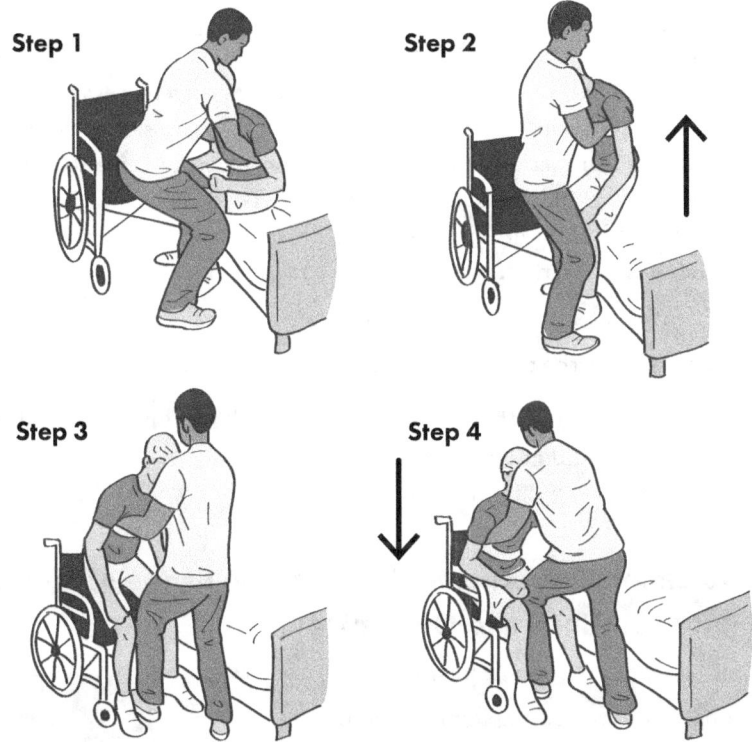

Figure 1.10. Transferring Patient from Bed to Wheelchair

Skills Evaluation: Position on Side

1. Lower the head of the bed.
2. Raise rail on the side of the bed the patient will turn toward.
3. Ask patient to reach for the side rail if able, while assisting them to slowly roll onto their side.
4. Place pillow under patient's head.
5. Reposition patient's shoulder and arm so patient is not laying on arm.
6. Place pillow behind client's back.

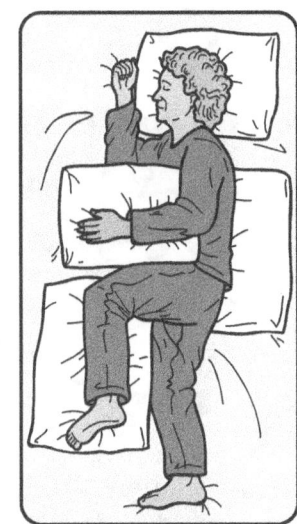

Figure 1.11. Supportive Devices Used in Side Position

7. Bend patient's knee and place pillow between their legs and under knee and ankle for support.
8. Wash hands.

QUICK REVIEW QUESTION

15. If a patient complains of pain while being transferred from a bed to a wheelchair, the nurse aide SHOULD:
    A) tell the patient they will document the pain in the patient's chart.
    B) ignore the patient's complaint and continue the transfer.
    C) immediately stop the transfer and return the patient to bed.
    D) try to complete the transfer using a different procedure.

Range of Motion Exercises

Range of motion (ROM) exercises are the movement of extremities through the full range of their natural motion (without causing pain). ROM exercises strengthen muscles and prevent muscle degradation caused by lack of movement. **Active ROM exercises** can be done by the patient alone. During **passive ROM exercises**, the nurse aide moves the limb through the ROM with little or no help from the patient. General guidelines for ROM exercises are given below.

- Move patient's limbs slowly and gently at joints to prevent injury.
- Only move as far as the patient is able to do so comfortably.
- Support limbs at joints (elbows and wrist for arms, knees and ankles for legs).
- ROM exercises should never be forced. If the patient experiences pain or discomfort, stop exercise immediately.

HELPFUL HINT
Abduction is movement of a limb away from the body.
Adduction is the movement of a limb toward the body.

Skills Evaluation: Perform Modified Passive Range of Motion (PROM) for One Knee and One Ankle

1. Place patient in the supine position.
2. Ask patient to voice complaints of pain.

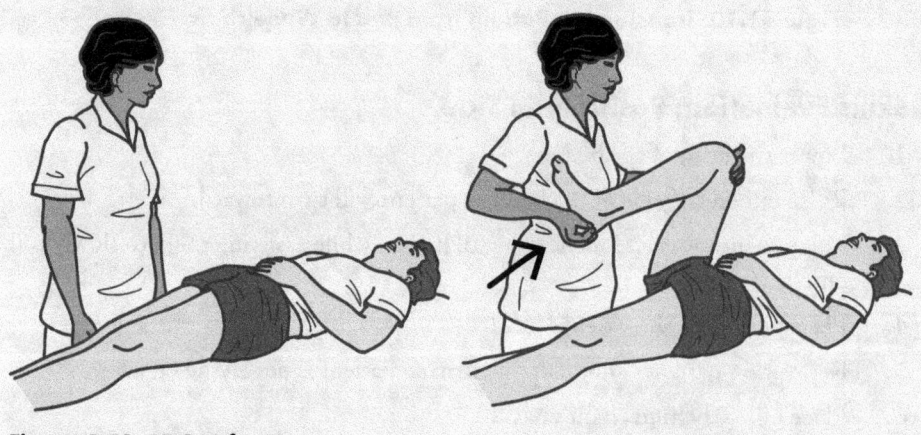

Figure 1.12. PROM for Knee

3. Support leg at knee and ankle and gently bend and straighten patient's leg at the knee three times. (Stop exercise if patient complains of pain.)
4. Lift patient's foot a few inches off the bed, supporting their ankle, and push/pull foot three times. (Stop exercise if patient complains of pain.)
5. Wash hands.

Skills Evaluation: Perform Modified Passive Range of Motion (PROM) for One Shoulder

1. Instruct patient to voice complaints of pain.
2. Support arm at elbow and wrist, and gently lift straight arm up toward the patient's head until it is level with their ear. Repeat three times. (Stop exercise if patient complains of pain.)
3. Support arm at elbow and wrist, and gently lift straight arm away from the patient's body until it reaches shoulder level. Repeat three times. (Stop exercise if patient complains of pain.)
4. Wash hands.

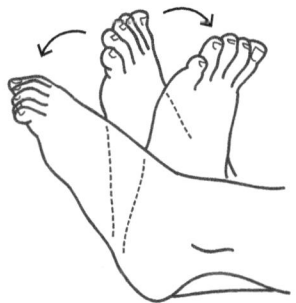

Figure 1.13. PROM for Ankle

Figure 1.14. PROM for Shoulder

QUICK REVIEW QUESTION

16. When performing passive ROM exercises for the knee, the patient should be:
    A) supine.
    B) prone.
    C) sitting on the edge of the bed.
    D) standing next to a chair.

ANSWER KEY

1. **B) is correct.** Clean dentures should be put in a cup of water or solution and placed within reach of the patient.
2. **C) is correct.** The nurse aide should start a tub bath by washing the client's eyes, then moving outward to the rest of the face.
3. **A) is correct.** To remove the top sheet from an occupied bed, the nurse aide should drape the patient with a bath blanket and remove the top sheet from underneath. This allows the patient to remain covered.
4. **B) is correct.** Clothing should be removed starting with the stronger side.
5. **D) is correct.** When the nurse aide notices any change in skin condition, including sores on the scalp, they should notify the nurse.
6. **C) is correct.** The nurse aide should apply pressure to the wound to prevent further bleeding and immediately notify the nurse.
7. **A) is correct.** Diets that are high in fiber can help relieve constipation.
8. **A) is correct.** Patients who are NPO should not eat or drink. The nurse aide should tell the patient they cannot give them a lunch tray and alert the nurse so she can talk with the patient.
9. **C) is correct.** When assisting clients with eating, fluids should be offered regularly throughout the meal to help patients chew and swallow foods.
10. **A) is correct.** Moisture barrier cream is used with incontinence products to help prevent skin damage caused by moisture and bacteria.
11. **D) is correct.** To reconnect a drainage tube to an indwelling catheter, the end of the drainage tube should be wiped with antiseptic to prevent infection.
12. **D) is correct.** After receiving an enema, patients will need to defecate. The nurse aide should be prepared to assist the patient with a bedpan or commode, or to move them to the toilet.
13. **B) is correct.** The nurse aide should show sympathy to the patient. The nurse aide cannot change the patient's schedule on their own, but they can offer to speak to the nurse about it.
14. **C) is correct.** The patient's sedation level will be monitored by a nurse.
15. **C) is correct.** Moves and transfers should be stopped for any new complaints of pain. In addition, the nurse should be notified so modifications can be made to the care plan.
16. **A) is correct.** Passive ROM exercises for the knee are done with the patient supine in the bed.

TWO: BASIC NURSING SKILLS

The Physical Exam

The purpose of the patient **physical examination** is to assess the patient's health. The nurse aide's role in the physical exam may include preparing the room, greeting the patient, and taking vital signs. Specific tasks may include:

- collecting necessary equipment
- escorting the patient to the exam room
- positioning and draping/gowning the patient
- assisting with the exam (e.g., providing equipment)
- disposing of used equipment
- cleaning the exam room

During this process, the nurse aide should provide the patient with a sense of support and security. The nurse aide should explain each step to the patient and provide for their privacy (e.g., closing curtains).

QUICK REVIEW QUESTION

1. When an alert and mobile patient needs to be draped for an exam, the nurse aide should:
    A) position the drape on the patient after they have undressed.
    B) instruct the patient on how to position the drape and leave the room while they undress.
    C) ask the nurse to place the drape on the patient.
    D) leave the door open to ensure the patient has placed the drape correctly.

Positioning Patients

The medical assistant should position the patient appropriately for different types of exams. These positions are discussed in Table 2.1.

Table 2.1. Medical Examination Positions

Position	Description
Lateral	Patient is lying on side with right side on the bed (right lateral) or left side on the bed (left lateral). Pillows are placed behind the patient's back and under the knee, head, and neck. Lateral position is used for patient comfort and to prevent injuries from long-term bedrest.
Supine	Patient lies on their back with arms to the sides. Supine positions are used during many surgical procedures, while performing an ECG, and for obtaining orthostatic blood pressure.
Dorsal recumbent	Patient lies on their back with knees bent and feet flat on the table. Dorsal recumbent positions are used for gynecological exams.
Lithotomy	Patient lies on their back with buttocks on the edge of the lower end of the table, legs elevated, and feet in stirrups. Lithotomy position is used for gynecological exams, childbirth, and some surgeries.
Sims	Patient lies on their left side with the left leg flexed, left arm resting behind the body, right leg flexed, and right arm at the chest. Sims position is used for taking the temperature rectally, rectal examinations, and administering enemas.
Prone	Patient lies on their stomach. Prone position is used to examine the spine and for chiropractic procedures.
Fowler's	Patient lies faceup with their upper body elevated at 45 to 60 degrees. Fowler's position is used in barium swallow procedures, nasopharyngeal feedings, and respiratory distress.
Semi-Fowler's	Same as Fowler's position, except the upper body is only elevated between 30 and 45 degrees. Semi-Fowler's position is used for nasogastric feedings, X-rays, and respiratory distress.

QUICK REVIEW QUESTION

2. The nurse has asked the nurse aide to place a patient in Fowler's position. The nurse aide should position the head of the bed:
    A) flat.
    B) at a 30° angle.
    C) at a 45° angle.
    D) at a 90° angle.

Vital Signs

BODY TEMPERATURE

Body temperature can be measured with a thermometer by various routes (see Table 2.2). Elevated temperature, or **fever**, is defined as a temperature higher than 100.4°F (38°C) (although this is not a universal standard—some physicians may use a different cutoff temperature). **Hypothermia** (body temperature below 95°F or 35°C) can occur when the body is exposed to cold weather or due to medical conditions such as a thyroid disorder.

HELPFUL HINT
Rectal temperature is taken with the patient in Sims position.

Table 2.2. Measuring Body Temperature

Method	Location	Baseline
Axillary	armpit	97.6°F (36.5°C)
Oral	under tongue	98.6°F (37.0°C)
Rectal	rectum	99.6°F (37.5°C)
Temporal artery	forehead	99.6°F (37.5°C)
Tympanic membrane	inside ear	98.6°F (37.0°C)

QUICK REVIEW QUESTION

3. To take a patient's temperature at the temporal artery, the nurse aide should place the thermometer:
   A) in the ear.
   B) in the rectum.
   C) on the forehead.
   D) under the tongue.

PULSE

The **pulse**, or **heart rate**, is the number of times the heart beats per minute. The average adult's pulse rate at rest is between 60 and 100 beats per minute. The pulse can be taken at a number of locations on the body.

- carotid pulse: to the side of the trachea
- radial pulse: on the thumb side of the inner wrist
- brachial pulse: on the side of the crease of the elbow
- pedal pulse: on the top of the foot
- apical pulse: at the apex of the heart (with stethoscope)

HELPFUL HINT
Heart rate can also be found on the readouts of equipment used to test cardiovascular performance, including pulse oximeters and electrocardiograms (ECGs).

Skills Evaluation: Counts and Records Radial Pulse

1. Explain procedure to patient.
2. Locate radial pulse with fingertips.
3. Count the beats for 1 minute.

BASIC NURSING SKILLS

4. Wash hands.
5. Record pulse.

Note: To pass this skill, you will need to record a pulse rate within 4 beats of the rate recorded by the evaluator.

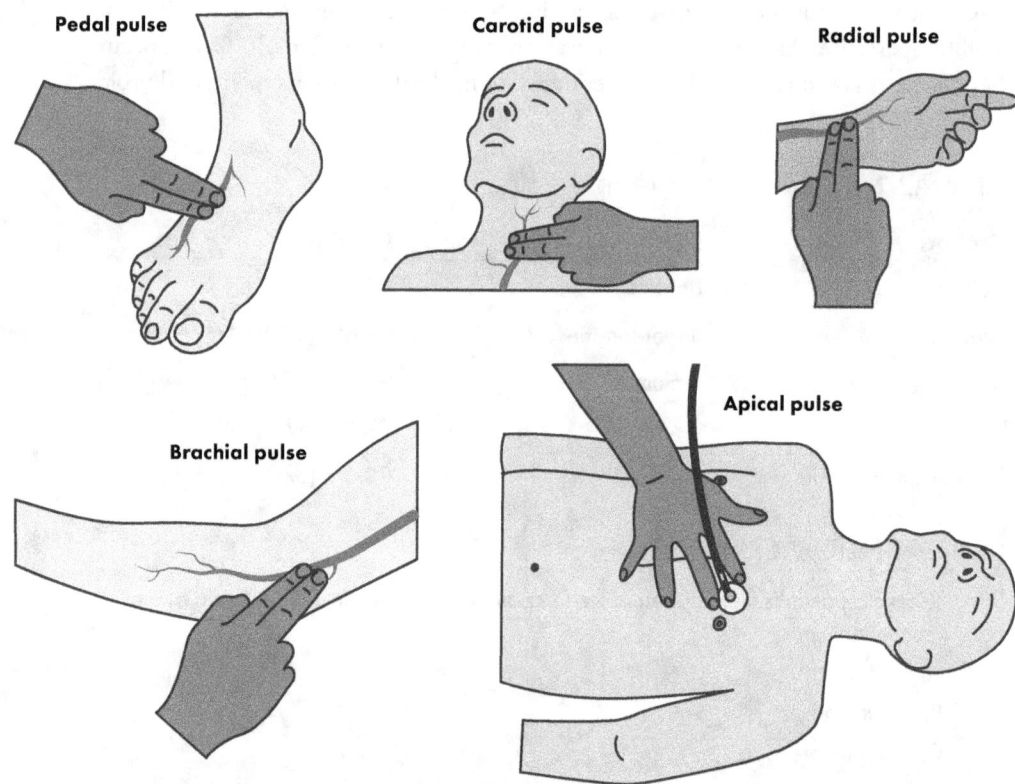

Figure 2.1. Locations for Measuring Pulse Rate

QUICK REVIEW QUESTION

4. The carotid pulse can be palpated at which of the following locations on the body?
   A) the anterior wrist
   B) lateral to the trachea
   C) in the groin
   D) on the dorsum of the foot

RESPIRATORY RATE

A person's **respiratory rate (RR)** is the number of breaths taken per minute. Respiratory rate is usually found by having the patient lie on their back (although this is not required) and counting the rise and fall of their chest. For an accurate measurement, the patient should be allowed to rest before the respiratory rate is measured. A normal adult's RR is 12 to 20 breaths per minute, although this rate can vary in children and adults over 65.

Skills Evaluation: Counts and Records Respirations

1. Explain procedure to patient.
2. Count patient's respirations for 1 minute.
3. Wash hands.
4. Record respirations.

Note: To pass this skill, you will need to record a rate within 2 breaths of the rate recorded by the evaluator.

QUICK REVIEW QUESTION

5. What position should a patient be in when the nurse aide measures respiratory rate?
   A) Sims
   B) lateral
   C) prone
   D) supine

BLOOD PRESSURE

Blood pressure (BP) is the measurement of the force of blood as it flows against the walls of the arteries. BP is measured in mm Hg (millimeters of mercury). Blood pressure is written as two numbers: systolic pressure and diastolic pressure. **Systolic pressure** is the pressure that occurs while the heart is contracting; **diastolic pressure** occurs while the heart is relaxed.

A healthy blood pressure has a systolic value of 100 to 139 mm Hg and a diastolic value of 60 to 79 mm Hg. High blood pressure is called **hypertension**; low blood pressure is **hypotension**.

Blood pressure can be taken manually using a blood pressure cuff and stethoscope or by using an automatic or semiautomatic blood pressure monitor. (Both the cuff and electronic monitors are referred to as **sphygmomanometers**.) For both methods, the patient should be upright, with their feet on the floor and uncrossed, and the arm being used for the measurement should be at heart height.

systolic pressure
↑
$$\frac{120}{80} \text{ mm Hg}$$
↓
diastolic pressure

Figure 2.2. Systolic and Diastolic Blood Pressure

HELPFUL HINT
Korotkoff sounds occur as the BP cuff is deflated. The first sound is the systolic pressure, and the last (fifth) sound is the diastolic pressure.

Skills Evaluation: Measures and Records Manual Blood Pressure

1. Explain procedure to patient.
2. Wipe stethoscope with alcohol.
3. Position patient with palm up and locate brachial artery.
4. Place cuff on client's upper arm with sensor over brachial artery.
5. Position stethoscope over brachial artery.
6. Inflate cuff between 160 mm Hg and 180 mm Hg. (If sounds are heard immediately, deflate cuff and reinflate to 200 mm Hg.)
7. Note systolic pressure (first sound) and diastolic pressure (last sound).
8. Remove cuff.

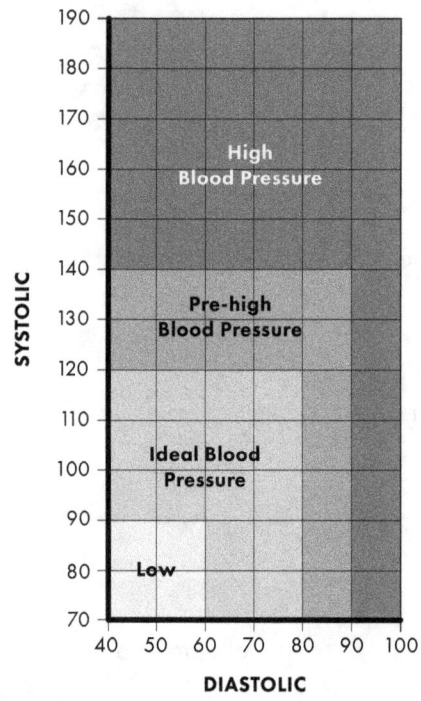

Figure 2.3. Classifying Blood Pressure

9. Wash hands.
10. Record BP.

Note: To pass this skill, you will need to record a systolic and diastolic BP within 2 mm Hg of the BP found by the evaluator.

To use an automatic blood pressure monitor, the nurse aide wraps the cuff around the patient's upper arm and turns on the monitor. It will automatically inflate, deflate, and provide a pressure reading. A semiautomatic monitor requires manual inflation but will automatically deflate and provide a pressure reading.

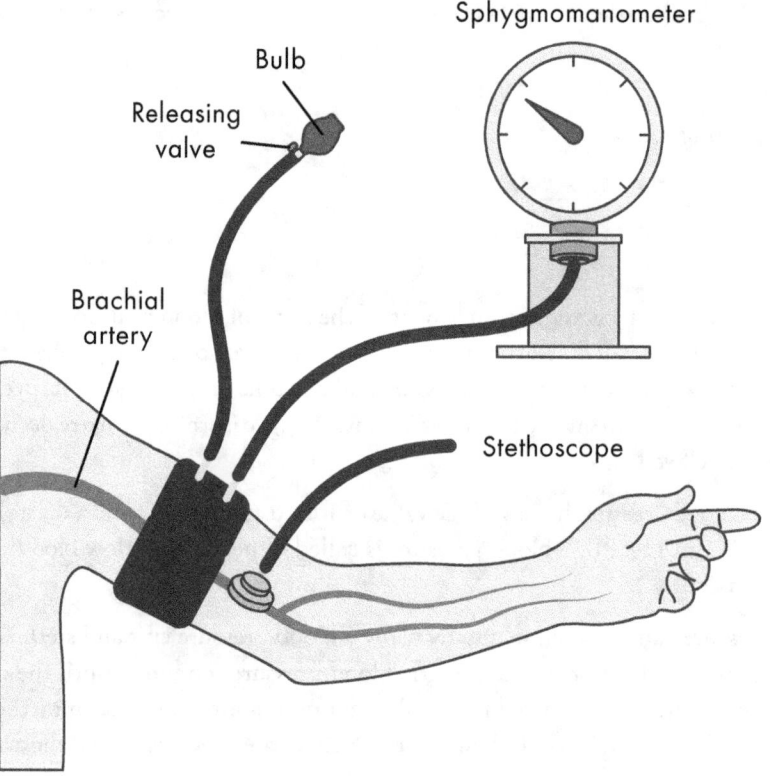

Figure 2.4. How to Take a Manual Blood Pressure Reading

QUICK REVIEW QUESTION

6. When using a sphygmomanometer to take a manual blood pressure, where is the stethoscope most commonly placed?
    A) carotid pulse
    B) dorsalis pedis pulse
    C) radial pulse
    D) brachial pulse

HEIGHT AND WEIGHT

The patient's **height** is assessed by using a fixed bar on the weight scale or wall. Height measurements are recorded in feet (ft) and inches (in) or in centimeters (cm).

The patient's **weight** is measured using a balanced scale and recorded in pounds (lb) or kilograms (kg). To convert between units for height and weight, multiply using the conversion factors given in Table 2.3.

Table 2.3. Converting Units

Original unit	Operation	New unit
Pounds	divide by 2.2	kilograms
Kilograms	multiply by 2.2	pounds
Inches	multiply by 2.54	centimeters
Centimeters	divide by 2.54	inches

12 inches = 1 foot
100 cm = 1 meter
16 ounces = 1 pound

Skills Evaluation: Measures and Records Weight of Ambulatory Client

1. Explain procedure to patient.
2. Ensure patient is wearing nonskid footwear.
3. Set scale to zero.
4. Ask client to step on scale and read the weight.
5. Ask client to step off scale.
6. Wash hands.
7. Record weight.

Note: To pass this skill, you will need to record a weight within 2 pounds (0.9 kg) of the weight found by the evaluator.

QUICK REVIEW QUESTION

7. According to the scale, an infant weighs 4.3 kg. What is the infant's weight in pounds?
   A) 1.95 lbs
   B) 5.2 lbs
   C) 8.6 lbs
   D) 9.46 lbs

OXYGEN SATURATION AND PULSE OXIMETRY

Oxygen saturation is a measurement of the amount of oxygen in the blood. Specifically, it measures the amount of oxygen-saturated hemoglobin (the substance in red blood cells that carries oxygen) relative to unsaturated hemoglobin. Normal blood oxygen level is 94 to 100 percent. Oxygen saturation is measured using a **pulse oximeter**, which is usually placed on the patient's finger. When the patient's finger is not accessible, the oximeter can be placed on the big toe or earlobe.

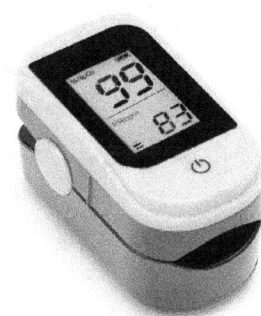

Figure 2.5. Pulse Oximeter

QUICK REVIEW QUESTION

8. Pulse oximetry can be measured on a patient at all of the following locations EXCEPT:

   A) a finger.
   B) the abdomen.
   C) the big toe.
   D) an earlobe.

Specimen Collection and Testing

URINE AND STOOL

Urine can be used to test for a wide variety of conditions, including pregnancy, infections, metabolic disorders (e.g., diabetes), organ dysfunction, and cancers. Urine can be collected at random times or at a specific time.

- **Random** urine samples are not taken at a scheduled time.
- A **first morning** urine sample is collected before the patient takes in any fluid so that the urine is more concentrated (usually after 8 hours of sleep).
- A **timed** urinalysis can span 2 to 72 hours. (A 24-hour specimen is the most common.)
  - Urine is collected over the given time period and added to a large collection container.
  - The patient should discard their first morning urine and start collecting urine after that.

HELPFUL HINT

Urinary collection bags are used to collect urine samples from pediatric patients. The adhesive bag is sealed around the baby's genitals and removed once enough urine has been collected.

Most urine samples are **voided** (passed from the body). A **regular voided sample** can be collected by the patient without any special preparations. **Double voiding** requires the patient to discard their first morning urine and wait a set amount of time (usually 30 minutes) to collect a sample. A **midstream clean catch** is collected after the perianal region has been cleaned with an antiseptic wipe and the patient has already voided a small amount of urine.

Skills Evaluation: Measures and Records Urinary Output

1. Put on gloves.
2. Pour urine from bedpan into measuring container.
3. Rinse bedpan and pour rinse water into toilet.
4. Measure urine in container.
5. Empty measuring container into toilet.
6. Rinse measuring container and pour rinse water into toilet.
7. Remove gloves and wash hands.
8. Record urine amount.

Note: To pass this skill, you will need to record a volume within 25 mL of the volume found by the evaluator.

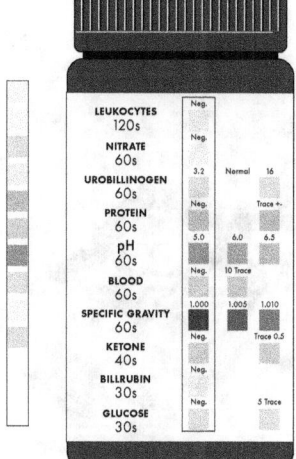

Figure 2.6. Urine Dipstick Container

The chemical component of urinalysis (U/A) can be done at point of care using a urine **dipstick** that is placed in a urine sample. The reagent pads on the dipstick change color when components being tested for are present. The dipstick can be read by comparing it to the color chart provided by the manufacturer.

Stool (fecal) samples are collected to test for disorders of the gastrointestinal (GI) system, including infections, cancers, and bleeding. **Fecal occult blood tests** (also called guaiac tests or guaiac smears) are a common test for occult (hidden) blood. Occult blood may be present if the patient has a GI disorder such as colorectal cancer or ulcerative colitis.

Stool samples may be collected in a large container placed inside the toilet. For smaller samples, the patient may use a scoop to place a small portion of feces in the collection container. The sample should be uncontaminated by urine.

QUICK REVIEW QUESTION

9. To collect a midstream clean catch urine specimen, the nurse aide should:
   A) collect the first voided urine.
   B) clean the perianal region with antiseptic before collecting the specimen.
   C) attach a urinary collection bag over the genital area.
   D) ensure that the patient has fasted for at least 8 hours before specimen collection.

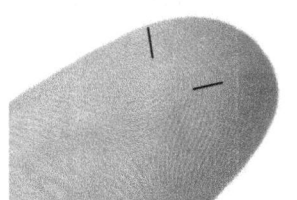

Figure 2.7. Stool Sample Collection Devices

GLUCOSE

Glucose levels in the blood can be tested at the point of care with small, portable glucose meters. A **lancet** is used to puncture the skin, and a small amount of blood is placed on the test strip. The meter then provides a readout of the glucose level. Important considerations for skin punctures include:

- In adults, use the side of the middle or ring finger.
- In infants, puncture the heel.
- Puncture skin perpendicular to fingerprint lines.
- Wipe away the first drop of blood before collecting the sample.
- Never do a skin puncture at the site of a previous puncture or at a site that is bruised or swollen.
- Do not use povidone-iodine for skin puncture.

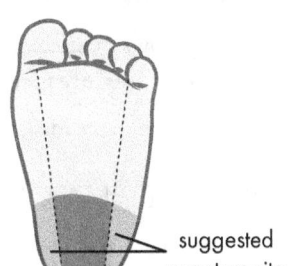

Figure 2.8. Location of Finger Stick and Heel Stick

HELPFUL HINT
Normal blood glucose levels are 70 – 100 mg/dL.

QUICK REVIEW QUESTION

10. When testing glucose levels on an adult, the skin should be punctured on the:
    A) side of the middle finger.
    B) middle of the heel.
    C) palm of the nondominant hand.
    D) the big toe.

BASIC NURSING SKILLS

Wounds

A **wound** is a break in the skin. They may be caused by trauma, pressure, or underlying medical conditions (e.g., lack of blood flow). Wounds are classified based on the type of damage done to the skin.

- A **contusion** is a bruise caused by impact with a hard surface.
- An **abrasion** is scraping or rubbing of the skin.
- A **laceration** is a cut through the skin.
- A **skin tear** occurs when the top layer of the skin is pulled away.
- An **ulcer** is a sore caused by the disintegration of the skin and underlying tissue.
  - **Circulatory ulcers** are caused by lack of blood flow to the affected area.
  - **Diabetic foot ulcers** are a common complication of diabetes.
  - **Pressure ulcers** are caused by continued pressure on a localized area.

Some patients, including those who are over 65 years old, malnourished, or have underlying medical conditions, are at high risk of receiving wounds during medical care. Nurse aides must take preventive measures to avoid causing wounds. They will also provide care to maintain skin integrity and prevent wounds (particularly ulcers). General wound prevention guidelines are given below.

- Provide skin care to keep skin clean and dry.
  - Bathe gently with an appropriate cleanser and pat dry.
  - Apply moisturizer to dry areas.
  - Change linens and provide barriers as needed for incontinent patients.
- Use appropriate padding and lift devices to avoid skin tears when transferring and positioning patients.
- Be cautious when removing tape or dressings.
- Reposition patients regularly (per care plan) to avoid pressure ulcers.
- Do not leave patients on equipment (e.g., bedpan, tubing) longer than necessary.
- Use pillows or specialized devices to prevent contact pressure on bony areas prone to pressure ulcers (e.g., heels, hips).
- Report changes in skin (e.g., redness, blisters) to nurse immediately.

QUICK REVIEW QUESTION

11. A patient restrained in the prone position is at high risk for developing pressure ulcers on the:
    A) inner knee.
    B) back of knee.
    C) heel.
    D) hip.

Restraints

Restraints are devices that restrict the patient's movement. They may be used to manage patients with medical symptoms that pose a threat to the patient or caregivers. Use of restraints requires approval from a physician or a nurse (in an emergency only), and the details of restraint use must be included in the care plan.

The nurse aide may be asked to monitor restrained patients. Patients should be checked at least every 15 minutes (per the care plan) to ensure that their airway, breathing, and circulation are not compromised. Every 2 hours, the patient should be released from the restraints so their personal and hygiene needs can be met (e.g., eating, elimination). Vital signs should also be taken. When reapplying restraints, the patient should be repositioned to avoid pressure ulcers or other position-related injuries.

HELPFUL HINT

Restraints should *never* be used to punish the patient or for the convenience of the nurse aide.

QUICK REVIEW QUESTION

12. A nurse aide has been asked to provide care for a patient who has just had wrist restraints removed. The nurse aide should do all of the following EXCEPT:
    A) tell the patient that if they cooperate the restraints will not be reapplied.
    B) help the patient with elimination needs.
    C) offer the patient fluids and food.
    D) take the patient's vital signs and assess the skin on the wrist.

ANSWER KEY

1. **B) is correct.** The nurse aide should respect the patient's privacy. If a patient is able to apply the drape, the aide should show them how to use it and allow them to undress and drape themselves.

2. **C) is correct.** In Fowler's position, the head of the bed is positioned between a 45° and 60° angle.

3. **C) is correct.** A temporal artery thermometer is used by sliding the thermometer across the forehead.

4. **B) is correct.** The carotid pulse is palpable lateral to the trachea.

5. **D) is correct.** The patient should be on their back (supine) so the nurse aide can see the rise and fall of their chest.

6. **D) is correct.** The stethoscope is placed over the brachial pulse (near the antecubital fossa) as the cuff is inflated and then slowly deflated.

7. **D) is correct.** 1 kilogram is equal to 2.2 pounds.

8. **B) is correct.** The abdomen is not a dependable location to measure pulse oximetry.

9. **B) is correct.** To collect a midstream clean catch urine sample, the nurse aide should clean the perianal region with antiseptic, allow the patient to void a small amount of urine, and then collect the urine sample.

10. **A) is correct.** On adults, a lancet should be used to puncture the skin on the side of the middle or ring finger to collect blood for testing.

11. **C) is correct.** Patients in a prone position will experience pressure on their heels as their feet rest on the mattress.

12. **A) is correct.** The nurse aide does not control when restraints are applied and should not use the threat of restraints to gain the patient's cooperation.

THREE: SAFETY and INFECTION CONTROL

Infection Control

INFECTION CYCLE AND THE CHAIN OF INFECTION

The goal of **infection control** is to intervene in the chain of infection at the point where infection is most likely to occur in order to prevent its spread. **Infection** occurs when an organism establishes an opportunistic relationship with a host. Infections can be caused by many different infectious agents.

- **Bacteria** are single-celled prokaryotic organisms that are responsible for many common infections such as strep throat, urinary tract infections, and many food-borne illnesses.

- **Viruses** are composed of a nucleic acid (DNA or RNA) wrapped in a protein capsid. They invade host cells and hijack cell machinery to reproduce. Viral infections include the common cold, influenza, and human immunodeficiency virus (HIV).

- **Protozoa** are single-celled eukaryotic organisms. Protozoan infections include giardia (an intestinal infection) and African sleeping sickness.

- **Fungi** are a group of eukaryotic organisms that include yeasts, molds, and mushrooms. Common fungal infections are athlete's foot, ringworm, and oral and vaginal yeast infections.

- **Parasitic diseases** are caused by parasites that live in or on the human body and use its resources. Common human parasites include worms (e.g., tapeworms), flukes, and ectoparasites like lice and ticks, which live on the outside of the body.

Infections travel from person to person via the **chain of infection**. The chain starts with a causative organism (e.g., a bacteria or virus). The organism needs a **reservoir**, or place to live. The reservoir may be biological (e.g., people or animals), or it may be environmental. For example, in a medical office, equipment and office surfaces may act as reservoirs. In order to spread, the infectious agent needs a way to exit the reservoir, such as being expelled as droplets during a sneeze.

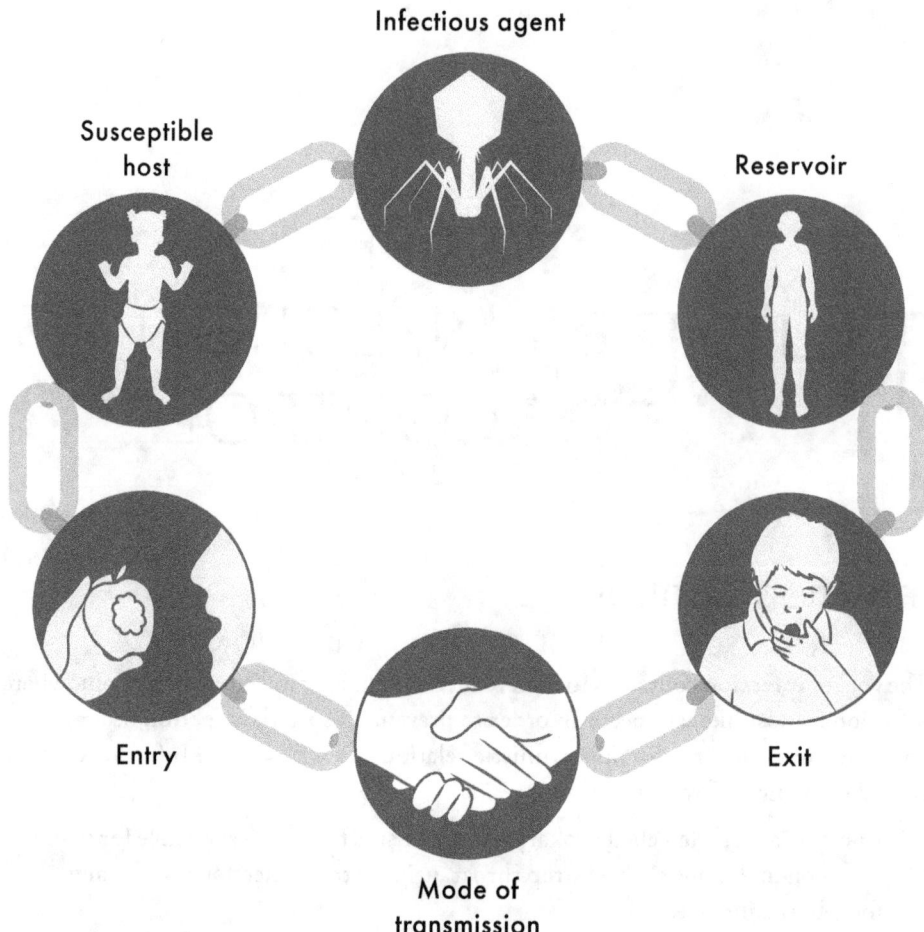

Figure 3.1. Chain of Infection

For the infection chain to continue, the infectious agent needs to encounter a susceptible **host**—a person who can become infected. Finally, the infectious agent needs a way to enter the host, such as through inhalation or drinking contaminated water. Infections may be transmitted to hosts via several modes of transmission.

- **Direct contact** is transmission from one infected person to another during physical contact with blood or other body fluids (e.g., transmission of herpes during sexual intercourse).
- **Indirect contact** is transmission of the disease through a nonbiological reservoir (e.g., drinking water contaminated with giardia).
- **Droplets** are infectious agents trapped in moisture that are expelled when an infected person sneezes or coughs. They can enter the respiratory system of other people and cause infection (e.g., transmission of influenza when an infected person sneezes).
- Some droplets are light enough to remain **airborne**, meaning people may inhale infectious agents from the air long after the initial cough or sneeze (e.g., measles, which can live in airborne droplets for up to two hours).
- Some diseases are carried by organisms called **vectors** that spread the disease; the infection does not require direct physical contact between people (e.g., mosquitoes carrying malaria).

HELPFUL HINT

Infectious disease precautions are categorized based on how the disease is transmitted. For example, droplet precautions require only a surgical mask, but airborne precautions require an N-95 respirator to prevent transmission.

QUICK REVIEW QUESTION

1. Which of the following is an example of transmission of an infectious agent through direct contact?
   A) kissing an infected person
   B) inhaling droplets from a sneezing infected person
   C) eating contaminated food
   D) inhaling microorganisms in the air

ASEPSIS

Asepsis is the absence of infectious organisms, and **medical asepsis** is the practice of destroying infectious agents outside the body to prevent the spread of disease. An object that has had all infectious agents removed or destroyed is **sterile**.

Medical asepsis is different from **clean technique**, which also aims to minimize the spread of infectious agents but does not require sterilization. Wearing gloves is an example of clean technique; the gloves are not sterile, but they provide a barrier that prevents the spread of infection from patient to provider.

The most important tool used for medical asepsis is handwashing. **Aseptic handwashing** is a specific technique intended to remove all infectious agents from the hands and wrists. Aseptic handwashing should be performed whenever the nurse aide is going to interact with a sterile field (e.g., when applying a sterile dressing).

HELPFUL HINT
Clean or sterile surfaces become **contaminated** when they come in contact with pathogens.

Skills Evaluation: Handwashing

1. Turn on water.
2. Wet hands and wrists.
3. Apply soap.
4. **Lather fingers, hands, and wrists for 20 seconds. (Keep hands lower than elbows and fingers down.)**
5. Clean fingernails on opposite palm.
6. **Rinse fingers, hands, and wrists. (Keep hands lower than elbows and fingers down.)**
7. Use clean towel to dry hands and dispose of towel.
8. Use clean towel or foot control to turn off faucet.

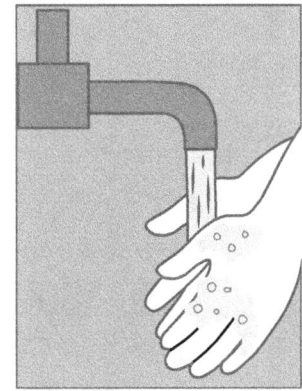

Figure 3.2. Handwashing Position

Medical asepsis also includes the removal of infectious agents from equipment and other surfaces. This process has three levels.

- **Cleaning** removes dirt and some infectious agents.
- **Disinfection** kills all pathogens except bacterial spores. Most surfaces in health care settings are disinfected using chemical agents such as alcohol or chlorine bleach.
- **Sterilization** kills all infectious agents, including bacterial spores. Medical equipment is sterilized using heat or chemicals (e.g., ethylene oxide).

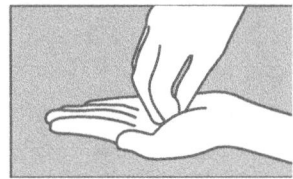

Figure 3.3. Cleaning Fingernails

SAFETY AND INFECTION CONTROL

Surgical asepsis is the practice of removing all infectious pathogens from all equipment involved in invasive procedures. Nurse aides may be asked to help sterilize equipment and may also be required to do a surgical scrub if participating in an invasive procedure. A **sterile field** is a work area free of contaminants.

QUICK REVIEW QUESTION

2. A surface is disinfected after it has been:
   A) cleaned with chlorine bleach.
   B) washed with soap and water.
   C) covered with a drape sheet.
   D) allowed to sit unused for 24 hours.

PERSONAL PROTECTIVE EQUIPMENT

In addition to handwashing, equipment can be used to prevent the spread of infection. **Personal protective equipment (PPE)** is any item necessary for the prevention of microorganism transmission. PPE includes gloves, gowns, goggles, eye shields, and masks. Some general guidelines for using PPE are given below.

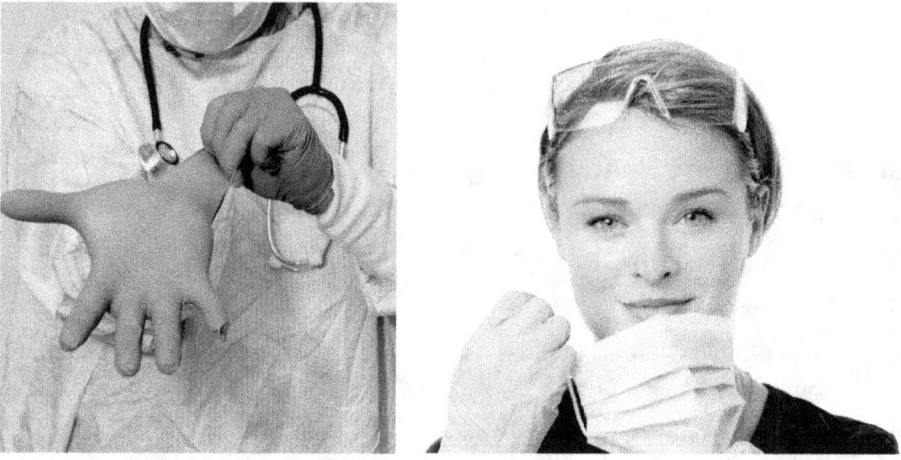

Figure 3.4. Personal Protective Equipment

- Wear gloves when the hands may contact bodily fluids, broken skin, or contaminated surfaces.
- Change contaminated gloves before touching a clean body site or clean equipment.
- Gloves must be discarded between each patient.
- The outside of gloves is contaminated; the inside of gloves is clean.
- Masks are used both to protect medical providers from splashes and to protect patients from infectious agents carried by the provider.
- Goggles and face shields are worn to protect the eyes, mouth, and nose from body fluid splashes.
- The order for putting on PPE is 1) gown, 2) mask, 3) goggles/face shield, 4) gloves.

- Remove all PPE except respirators before leaving the patient's room.
- Wash hands after removing PPE.

Skills Evaluation: Donning and Removing Gown and Gloves

1. Unfold gown and put arms through sleeves.
2. Fasten gown at neck and then at waist.
3. Put on gloves so that gloves cover gown cuff.
4. Remove gloves:
   a. Use one gloved hand to grasp other glove at the palm and remove.
   b. Slide ungloved fingers under the remaining glove cuff, and remove while turning glove inside out.
   c. Dispose of gloves.

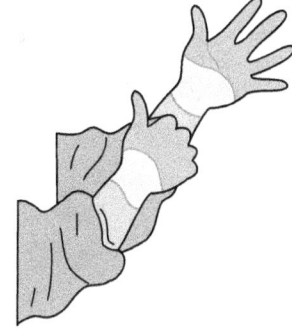

Figure 3.5. Positioning Gloves Over Gown Cuff

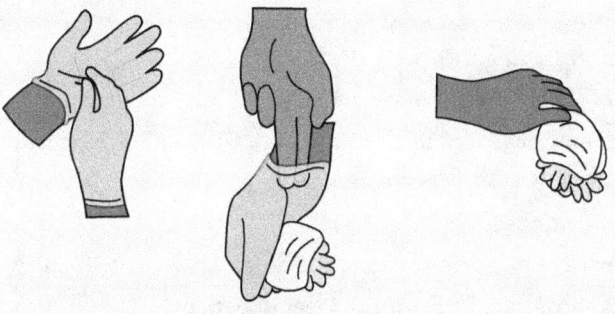

Figure 3.6. Removing Gloves

5. Untie and remove gown without touching contaminated area of gown.
6. Dispose of gown.
7. Wash hands.

QUICK REVIEW QUESTION

3. Which of the following statements about PPE is NOT correct?
   A) Hands do not need to be washed before putting on gloves.
   B) A face shield is worn when body fluid splashes are likely.
   C) Fluid-resistant gowns should be removed after leaving a patient's room.
   D) PPE devices include gloves, gowns, eye shields, and masks.

STANDARD PRECAUTIONS AND BLOOD-BORNE PATHOGEN STANDARDS

Standard precautions (also called universal precautions) are based on the assumption that all patients are infected with microorganisms, whether or not there are symptoms or a diagnosis. Standard precautions decrease the risk of transmission of microorganisms from blood and other body fluids. The standards apply to contact with blood, all body fluids, secretions, and excretions (except sweat), non-intact skin, and mucous membranes.

This set of principles is used by all health care workers who have direct or indirect contact with patients. When working with patients and specimens, the nurse aide should always follow these standard precautions:

- Assume that all patients are carrying a microorganism.
- Use appropriate PPE.
- Practice hand hygiene.
- Follow needle-stick prevention policies.
- Clean and disinfect surfaces after each patient.
- Use disposable barriers to protect surfaces that are hard to disinfect.

HELPFUL HINT
Hand hygiene: Use soap and water when hands are visibly soiled. Antimicrobial foam or gel may be used if hands are not visibly soiled.

Additional precautions may be needed for patients with known infections. These precautions are based on the transmission route for the infection.

- Airborne precautions:
  o Wear N-95 respirator mask; place on before entering the room and keep on until after leaving the room.
  o Place N-95 or surgical mask on patient during transport.
  o Patient may be placed in a private room with a negative-pressure air system with the door kept closed.
- Droplet precautions:
  o Place patient in a private room; the door may remain open.
  o Wear appropriate PPE within 3 feet of patient.
  o Wash hands with antimicrobial soap after removing gloves and mask and before leaving the patient's room.
  o Place surgical mask on patient during transport.
- Contact precautions:
  o Place the patient in a private room; the door may remain open.
  o Wear gloves.
  o Change gloves after touching infected materials.
  o Remove gloves before leaving patient's room.
  o Wear gown; remove before leaving patient's room.
  o Use patient-dedicated equipment if possible; clean and disinfect community equipment between patients.
  o During transport, keep precautions in place and notify different areas or departments as needed.

QUICK REVIEW QUESTION

4. The use of standard precautions is NOT required for contact with:
   A) blood.
   B) urine.
   C) sweat.
   D) vomit.

BIOHAZARD DISPOSAL AND REGULATED WASTE

Regulated medical waste (RMW) (also called biohazardous waste) is any waste that is or may be contaminated with infectious materials, including blood, secretions, and excretions. Regulated medical waste must be handled carefully to prevent the possibility of an exposure incident. The disposal of RMW is governed by federal, state, and local regulations that vary by location. Some general waste disposal guidelines are given below.

- Sharps should be disposed of in a **biohazard sharps container**. The term "sharps" refers to needles, lancets, blood tubes, capillary tubes, razor blades, suturing needles, hypodermic needles, and microscope slides and coverslips.
- Blood and body fluids, such as urine, sputum, semen, amniotic fluid, and cerebrospinal fluid, can be disposed of in a drain, toilet, or utility sink. State and local regulations may limit the amount of fluid that can be disposed of into the sewage system.
- Feces should be flushed in a toilet.
- Bandages, dressing gauzes, and gloves with small amounts of RMW can be put in regular garbage disposal cans.
- Dirty linen should be put in a separate receptacle; if very soiled by blood or infectious material, it should be put in a biohazard bag.
- Chemicals should be stored and disposed of according to the information in the **safety data sheets (SDSs)**, which are provided by the manufacturer.

Spill kits are a collection of substances and PPE that assist in cleaning and containing infectious agents or chemical agents after a spill. Spill kits may be general purpose, or they may be tailored to a specific substance (e.g., mercury or body fluids).

QUICK REVIEW QUESTION

5. A patient diagnosed with *C. diff* has soiled the bed, and the nurse aide is stripping the bed. The nurse aide should:
   A) throw the linens in the trash can.
   B) place the linens in a red biohazard bag.
   C) place the soiled linens in a regular dirty linen bag.
   D) rinse the soiled linens before placing them in a soiled linen bag.

Emergency Response
EMERGENCY CARE

A **medical emergency** is an unexpected, life-threatening event. It can occur at any time, so it is important to be prepared and understand what to do. A nurse aide's role is to stay calm and follow the office's emergency management policy and protocol. The more prepared the nurse aide is for an emergency, the better the outcome will be for the patient. Knowing how to recognize common emergency situations and what to do can help ensure that the patient remains safe and the event does not escalate.

HELPFUL HINT

It is important that the nurse aide does not attempt to diagnose or independently treat any issues. If the nurse aide believes a patient has symptoms requiring urgent assessment or treatment, the appropriate medical provider should be notified immediately.

Some key points for the nurse aide to remember during an emergency are:

- Secure the scene and do not panic.
- Relocate nearby visitors and patients.
- Work with other members of the health care team to ensure that all necessary equipment is available.
- Know the location of the crash cart.
- Maintain cardiopulmonary resuscitation (CPR) certification and follow training.
- Do not attempt any intervention without the proper training.
- Be observant; the nurse aide may need to provide information about the event.
- Remember to complete all applicable documentation regarding the emergency.

Anaphylactic Shock

Anaphylactic shock (or anaphylaxis) is a life-threatening, severe allergic reaction that causes widening of blood vessels and constriction of airways in the lungs. The most common causes of anaphylactic shock are food allergens, medications, and insect venom. Symptoms of anaphylactic shock include:

- respiratory distress (can be severe)
- swelling (edema) in face, lips, or tongue
- skin pallor or flushing
- low blood pressure
- dizziness or fainting
- altered mental status

HELPFUL HINT
Many patients with allergies carry an EpiPen, which provides a premeasured dose of epinephrine for injection.

Anaphylactic shock is treated with an epinephrine injection. The provider may choose to transfer the patient to an emergency department for further observation or if treatment is ineffective.

Bleeding

There are three types of bleeding: arterial, venous, and capillary.

Arterial bleeding occurs when an artery is damaged. Because arteries carry high volumes of blood at high pressure, arterial bleeding can be life threatening and requires immediate intervention to prevent low blood pressure and other problems related to decrease in blood volume.

Arterial blood is bright red and "spurts" due to the pressure of the heart pumping. The blood is often moving too quickly for clotting to occur.

Venous bleeding occurs when a vein is damaged. Veins carry high volumes of blood, but they do not supply the same pressure as arteries, so although venous bleeding may be heavy, it is slower than arterial bleeding. The blood is also darker in color because it is deoxygenated.

Capillary bleeding occurs when the small blood vessels that create the network between veins and arteries are damaged. Capillary bleeding is often seen in wound beds or with skin abrasions. Bleeding from the capillaries is usually controlled easily.

The treatment for all types of bleeding is to apply direct pressure to the site.

1. Maintain standard precautions, including wearing gloves.
2. Place the patient in a prone position.
3. Apply pressure using sterile gauze. Pressure may be applied for up to 20 minutes depending on the type of bleed. If the bleed is arterial, pressure may be applied above the site of the bleeding (only if directed by the provider).
4. Assist with cleaning and dressing the wound once the bleeding has stopped.

> **HELPFUL HINT**
> Do not remove blood-soaked dressings, as this will interrupt the clotting process. Instead add gauze as necessary.

Cardiac and Respiratory Arrest

Cardiopulmonary (cardiac) arrest occurs when the heart stops beating, which causes blood flow to stop. The patient will have no pulse and either will not be breathing or will display labored breathing (agonal gasps). Immediately start cardiopulmonary resuscitation (CPR) for any patient in arrest.

Respiratory arrest occurs when breathing stops or is no longer effective at meeting the body's oxygen needs. Respiratory arrest often occurs with cardiac arrest but can occur alone as well. It will eventually lead to cardiac arrest.

Both cardiac and respiratory arrest are life-threatening conditions that require immediate treatment to preserve life and tissue function. The nurse aide should follow these steps:

1. Get help and contact 911.
2. Assess the patient and check for pulse (for no longer than five seconds). If the patient has a pulse, perform rescue breathing. If the patient has no pulse, begin performing CPR.

Rescue breathing:

- Use the head tilt–chin lift method to assess the airway.
- Ensure the patient's airway is clear.
- If an obstruction is visible, attempt to clear it. However, be careful to not obstruct the airway by pushing the object in deeper.
- Provide breaths at a rate of 10 to 12 breaths a minute.

CPR:

- Perform chest compressions at a rate of 30 compressions to two breaths for a single rescuer, with a goal of 100 compressions a minute.
- Compressions should be 2 inches in depth.
- Allow full chest recoil.
- Use the head tilt–chin lift method to assess the airway after the first 30 compressions.
- Use the automated external defibrillator (AED) as necessary.

Cerebrovascular Accident (CVA)

A **cerebrovascular accident (CVA)**, or **stroke**, occurs when the blood supply to the brain is disrupted due to damage in the brain's blood vessels. A **hemorrhagic stroke** occurs when a vessel ruptures in the brain. The blood that accumulates damages brain tissue and causes neurological impairment. An **ischemic stroke** occurs when arteries in the brain are blocked, leading to ischemia (reduced blood flow) and damage to brain tissue.

During a cerebrovascular event or stroke, response time is critical—the longer the CVA is untreated, the more damage will be done to the brain. The nurse aide should be able to recognize the symptoms of a stroke and communicate these to the provider. Patients may present with:

- unilateral face drooping
- arm weakness
- speech difficulty
- confusion
- severe headache

Foreign Body Obstruction

Choking is caused by a foreign body obstructing the airway. Unaddressed choking will lead to loss of consciousness and cardiac arrest. If a patient begins choking, the nurse aide should alert the nearest provider and attempt to dislodge the obstruction until a provider is available. Never perform a blind sweep, as this may lodge the object farther in the airway.

HELPFUL HINT
Choking is the most common cause of respiratory distress in pediatric patients.

If the patient is conscious, use the **Heimlich maneuver** or abdominal thrusts to dislodge the object. For an infant with an obstructed airway, the nurse aide should switch between five back slaps and five abdominal thrusts.

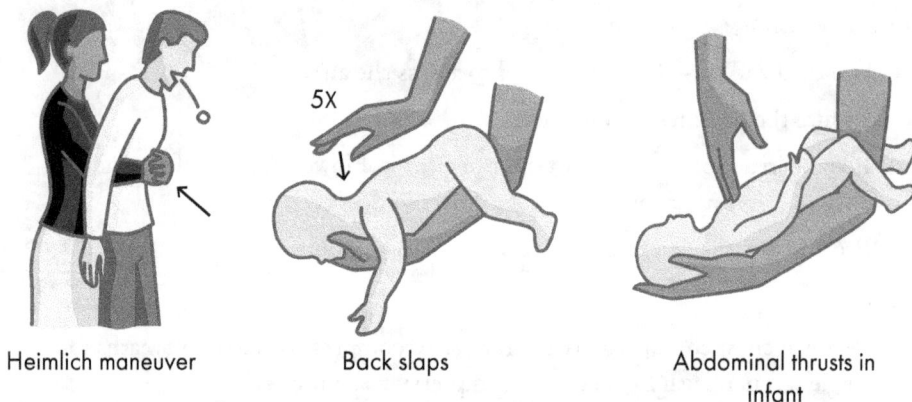

Heimlich maneuver   Back slaps   Abdominal thrusts in infant

Figure 3.7. Dislodging Foreign Bodies in Airway

Seizures

A **seizure** is caused by abnormal electrical discharges in the cortical gray matter of the brain; the discharges interrupt normal brain function. **Epilepsy** is a condition characterized by recurrent seizures.

Tonic-clonic seizures (a type of convulsive seizure) start with a tonic (contracted) state in which the patient stiffens and loses consciousness; this phase usually lasts less than one minute. The tonic phase is followed by the clonic phase, in which the patient's muscles rapidly contract and relax. The clonic phase can last up to several minutes.

During a seizure, the nurse aide should act to secure the safety of the patient:

- Remove any objects that might cause injury.
- Loosen tight clothing.
- Never restrain a seizing patient.
- Do not place anything in the patient's mouth.
- If needed, place the patient in the recovery position (on their side).
- Post-seizure patients are usually lethargic; allow recovery time.
- Ensure that the physician is aware of the situation.

Syncope

Syncope (fainting) is temporary partial or full loss of consciousness caused by decreased circulation of blood to the brain. Often syncope is in response to temperature changes, low blood pressure, fear or surprise, or low blood sugar. Symptoms that may precede an episode include flushing, dizziness, sweating, weakness, and paleness.

If the patient presents with syncopal symptoms, the nurse aide should make sure they are not in danger of falling by having them sit or lie down. The provider will conduct a full examination.

QUICK REVIEW QUESTION

6. A patient is having a tonic-clonic seizure. What should the nurse aide do first?
   A) Call 911.
   B) Restrain the patient.
   C) Take the patient's vital signs.
   D) Provide a safe environment.

EMERGENCY EQUIPMENT

It is important that an office have a crash cart or area where emergency equipment is easily accessible. Nurse aides should be familiar with the location of emergency equipment and how it is used. The nurse aide may be asked to retrieve or use supplies from the crash cart. The table below provides a list of common medical equipment that may be needed in an emergency.

Table 3.1. Common Emergency Medical Equipment

Equipment	Use
AED	restarts normal cardiac rhythm in patients with specific dysrhythmias
Portable oxygen tank	provides oxygen to patients with low oxygen saturation
Suction equipment	clears airways
Endotracheal tubes	opens airways and provides mechanical ventilation
CPR mask	covers patient's mouth during CPR
Bag-valve mask (this may have an oxygen hookup)	provides ventilation during cardiac or respiratory arrest

Table 3.1. Common Emergency Medical Equipment (continued)

Equipment	Use
Emergency medications	epinephrine: anaphylactic shock and cardiac arrest
	atropine: slow heart rate (bradycardia)
	sodium bicarb: high acid levels in blood and some types of overdoses
	activated charcoal: some poisonings
	ipecac: to induce vomiting
	aspirin: for patients experiencing acute coronary symptoms
IV supplies	for administration of fluids and medications
Dressings	for controlling bleeding and dressing wounds
PPE including gowns, gloves, surgical masks, and N-95 respirators	to prevent spread of infections

QUICK REVIEW QUESTION

7. A medical provider is caring for a patient in cardiac arrest. The nurse aide should anticipate that the provider may ask for:
   A) dressings.
   B) aspirin.
   C) a bag-valve mask.
   D) an N-95 respirator.

Fire and Electrical Safety

Although rare, fires in medical offices do occur. The nurse aide should be aware of certain fire safety measures:

- Keep open spaces free of clutter.
- Know the locations of fire exits, alarms, and extinguishers.
- Participate in fire drills, and know the evacuation plan of the health care facility.
- Do not use the elevator when a fire occurs.
- Turn off oxygen in the vicinity of a fire.
- Unplug electrical equipment that is malfunctioning or is near a fire.

Before use, electrical equipment should be inspected for defects and safety by checking three-pronged outlets and reading warning labels. Any electrical cords that are exposed, damaged, or frayed should be discarded, and circuits should not be overloaded. Safety measures include:

- Never run electrical wiring under carpets.
- Do not pull a plug by yanking the cord.
- Never use electrical appliances near bathtubs, sinks, or other water sources.

HELPFUL HINT
Water should never be used to put out electrical, grease, or chemical fires. The appropriate fire extinguisher should be used instead.

- Disconnect plugs from the outlet before cleaning appliances or equipment.

QUICK REVIEW QUESTION

8. The nurse aide should be prepared to perform all the following safety measures EXCEPT:

    A) participate in fire drills.

    B) remove candles from patient rooms.

    C) unplug malfunctioning equipment.

    D) use a fire extinguisher.

ANSWER KEY

1. **A) is correct.** Direct contact is the transmission of infectious agents through physical contact between two people, such as kissing.
2. **A) is correct.** Chlorine bleach is a disinfectant that will kill most pathogens.
3. **C) is correct.** Fluid-resistant gowns should be removed BEFORE leaving the patient's room to prevent spread of infection into the hallway.
4. **C) is correct.** Standard precautions are recommended whenever the nurse aide comes in contact with blood or body fluids that could transmit blood-borne pathogens. Blood-borne pathogens cannot be transmitted via sweat.
5. **B) is correct.** *C. diff* is highly contagious, and soiled linens require special handling. The nurse aide should place all linens in a red biohazard bag and put the bag in the designated area for biohazard bags in the soiled utility area.
6. **D) is correct.** Safety is the top priority during seizure activity, so the nurse aide should remove any objects in the immediate area that may cause the patient harm.
7. **C) is correct.** The patient in cardiac arrest requires CPR, and a bag-valve mask is used to deliver breaths during CPR.
8. **B) is correct.** The nurse aide should not take a patient's personal property. If the nurse aide has concerns about a patient's safety, they should alert the nurse.

FOUR: PSYCHOSOCIAL CARE SKILLS

Emotional, Spiritual, and Cultural Needs

Abraham Maslow's **hierarchy of needs** describes the needs that drive people's behavior. According to Maslow, as each stage is achieved, a person is encouraged to move to the next stage. The stages are often depicted as a pyramid: a person must meet the needs at the bottom of the pyramid before they can address needs at higher levels.

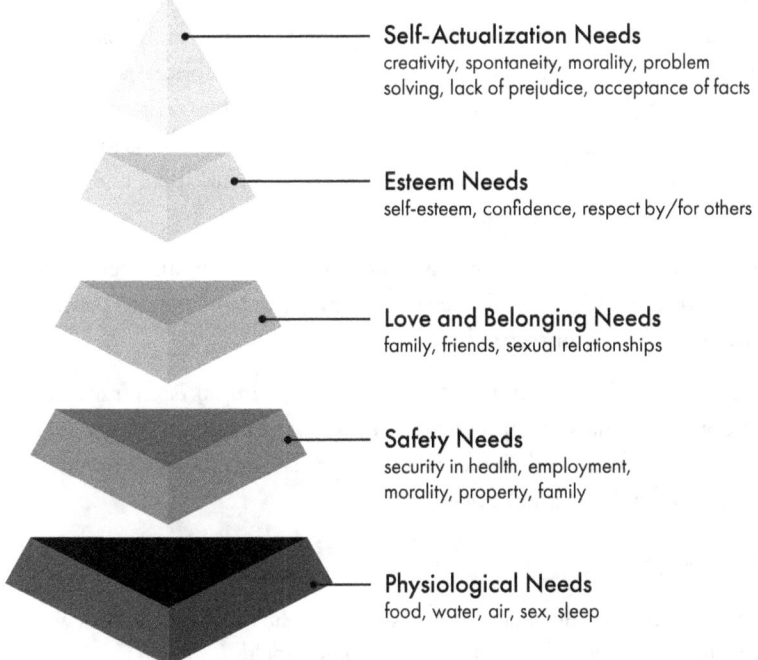

Figure 4.1. Maslow's Hierarchy of Needs

Patients will also have needs specific to their culture and spirituality. For example, patients may choose not to eat certain foods, or they may wish to attend religious services. These needs may be included in the care plan, or the patient may express them to the nurse aide. The nurse aide should respect patients' cultural and spiritual needs and should not ignore, judge, or challenge them.

HELPFUL HINT

If the patient's request interferes with care or the patient has needs the nurse aide cannot meet, the nurse aide should alert the nurse.

QUICK REVIEW QUESTION

1. A Muslim patient refuses to eat their lunch because it contains pork. The nurse aid should:
   A) tell the patient to only eat the foods that do not contain pork.
   B) take the food tray from the patient, and tell them they will get a different meal at dinner.
   C) explain to the patient that eating protein is important for health.
   D) alert the nurse that the patient needs to be brought a halal lunch.

Mental Health Needs

MENTAL HEALTH DISORDERS

The nurse aide should be able to recognize behaviors related to mental health disorders and be prepared to care for patients with altered behavior or mental status.

Delirium is a temporary cognitive change from baseline. The patient exhibits confusion and disorientation with a decreased ability to focus or hold attention. **Dementia** is a broad term for progressive, cognitively debilitating symptoms that interfere with independent functioning. Patients may show decline in one or more cognitive domains, including language, memory, executive function, motor skills, or social cognition. The most common cause of dementia is **Alzheimer's disease**.

A **situational crisis** is an acute change or event in a patient's life that may lead to feelings of anxiety, fear, depression, or other mental or emotional illness concerns (e.g., divorce, loss of a family member). **Suicidal ideation** is characterized by feelings or thoughts of attempting or considering suicide. Patients exhibiting suicidal ideation may have vague thoughts without a distinct plan, or they may have a specific plan and the means to carry it out.

Anxiety refers to feelings of fear, apprehension, and worry. Anxiety can be characterized as mild, moderate, or severe (panic). Anxiety will impact other functions such as the respiratory, cardiac, and gastrointestinal systems.

Bipolar disorder (formerly known as manic-depressive illness) is characterized by extreme shifts between mania and depression. **Mania** is a state of high energy, increased activity, and feelings of elation and immortality. **Depression** is a mood disorder characterized by feelings of sadness and hopelessness.

QUICK REVIEW QUESTION

2. A patient undergoing rehabilitation after a stroke tells the nurse aide that he would "rather die than keep living like this." The nurse aide should:
   A) encourage the patient not to give up on his rehabilitation program.
   B) alert the nurse that the patient has expressed suicidal ideation.
   C) ignore the patient's statement and continue his rehabilitation.
   D) ask the patient why he is depressed.

HELPFUL HINT

Altered behavior may be caused by a wide range of medical conditions, including hypoglycemia, stroke, head injury, and hypoxia (low oxygen). Sudden changes in a patient's behavior or mental status should always be reported to the nurse so the patient can be further assessed.

CARING FOR PATIENTS WITH ALTERED BEHAVIOR OR MENTAL STATUS

When communicating with patients with altered behavior or mental status, the nurse aide should always respect the patient and treat them with dignity and consideration. Speak in a slow, clear voice, and do not judge the patient or speak harshly. (See chapter 5 for more information on patient communication.)

Patients with dementia, delirium, or confusion require special care to meet their mental health needs. Some guidelines for caring for these patients are below.

- Do not challenge or affirm patients with delusions or hallucinations. Instead, redirect the conversation toward what is real.
- Do not argue with patients engaged in altered behavior (e.g., wandering, repetitive actions). Instead, keep them safe as they engage in these behaviors, and alert the nurse if intervention is needed.
- Follow routines and do not make changes to the environment.
- Use memory aids as described in the care plan.
- Explain procedures with simple, step-by-step instructions.
- Ensure the patient has access to items, activities, and people they enjoy or find soothing.

Patients with mental health disorders may become angry or violent. Mild aggression can be handled by the nurse aide, who can help address the cause, provide a soothing environment, or distract the patient. The nurse aide may also firmly ask the patient to stop the behavior. If the patient is abusive or violent, the nurse aide should prioritize their own safety and not try to manage the patient on their own. They may leave the room and then alert the nurse and security so they can safely manage the patient.

QUICK REVIEW QUESTION

3. A nurse aide is feeding a patient with Alzheimer's who tells the nurse aide that his wife is in the room. The nurse aide knows that the patient's wife recently died. The nurse aide should:

    A) ask the patient if he likes his meal and wants to keep eating.
    B) gently remind the patient that his wife is dead.
    C) alert the nurse that the patient is experiencing psychosis.
    D) ask the patient what his wife is saying.

ANSWER KEY

1. **D) is correct.** The nurse aide should respect the patient's religious needs. They should alert the nurse that the patient has requested a halal diet (which meets Muslim dietary restrictions). The patient can then be brought a new lunch, and the nurse can update the patient's care plan.

2. **B) is correct.** When a patient expresses suicidal thoughts, the nurse aide should alert the nurse as soon as possible so that the patient can receive the appropriate care.

3. **A) is correct.** Confusion is normal in patients with Alzheimer's. The nurse aide should not reinforce or challenge the patient's delusions and instead should focus the patient's attention on real, concrete behaviors.

FIVE: ROLE of the NURSE AIDE

Communication

Communication can be verbal or nonverbal. **Verbal communication** refers to words that are spoken or written. Guidelines for verbal communication are given in Table 5.1.

Table 5.1. Dos and Don'ts of Patient Communication

Do	Don't
Introduce yourself and use the patient's name.	Use medical jargon.
Speak directly to the patient when possible.	Threaten or intimidate the patient.
Speak slowly and clearly.	Lie or provide false hope.
Show empathy for the patient.	Interrupt the patient.
Be silent when appropriate to allow patients time to think and process emotions.	Show frustration or anger.
	Make judgmental statements.

Nonverbal communication includes all the physical aspects of communication, including posture, facial expression, and eye contact. Nurse aides should strive to keep their nonverbal communication professional and appropriate by:

- maintaining good posture (e.g., not slouching on a desk).
- keeping a polite facial expression when dealing with patients and the health care team.
- respecting other people's personal boundaries (e.g., not touching patients without their consent).
- maintaining eye contact when speaking with patients and the health care team.
- not using rude or inappropriate hand gestures.

Special communication techniques may be needed when working with diverse populations. Some of these guidelines are given in Table 5.2.

Table 5.2. Communicating with Diverse Populations

Population	Communication Techniques
Blind or low vision	Announce when you enter or leave the room. Address the patient by name. Describe the layout of the room. Narrate your actions.
Deaf or hard of hearing	Speak slowly and clearly. Allow the patient to see your face while you speak. Provide written materials. Use a sign language interpreter when needed.
Geriatric	Adjust language for confused or cognitively impaired patients. Rely on family members or caregivers as needed.
Pediatric	Move to patient's eye level. Use simple language. Explain exam procedures before you start. Allow patient to hold blunt, safe instruments.
Seriously or terminally ill	Respond promptly and allow patients any needed extra time. Be direct but kind. Do not offer false hope or make unfulfillable promises.
Intellectually disabled	Match the patient's level of vocabulary and sentence complexity. Speak directly to the patient.
Illiterate	Notice when patients do not read materials. Read or explain important documents.
Non-English speaking	Have materials available in multiple languages. Use an interpreter when needed.

QUICK REVIEW QUESTION

1. When questioning a patient through an interpreter, questions should be directed toward:
   A) the interpreter.
   B) the nurse.
   C) the patient's family.
   D) the patient.

Client Rights

Many different sets of **client rights** have been described by lawmakers and professional organizations. The two sets of client rights the nurse aide should be familiar with come from the American Hospital Association (AHA) and the Omnibus Budget Reconciliation Act of 1987 (OBRA).

The AHA formulated the **Patient's Bill of Rights** in 1973. This document outlines a patient's right to:

- receive respectful, considerate, and appropriate care.
- expect privacy and confidentiality.
- consult the physician of his or her choice.
- make decisions regarding health care.
- receive all information regarding diagnosis, treatment, and prognosis.
- refuse treatment.
- make informed decisions related to health care.
- obtain copies of his or her medical record.
- participate or refuse to participate in research.
- receive continuity of care.

In 2003, the AHA created the **Patient Care Partnership**. This brochure explains to patients what to expect during their hospital stay and outlines the hospital's responsibilities. The Patient Care Partnership outlines six key rights for all patients:

- high-quality hospital care
- clean and safe environment
- involvement in care
- protection of privacy
- help when leaving the hospital
- help with billing claims

The Omnibus Budget Reconciliation Act of 1987 (OBRA) outlines the rights held by residents of nursing centers. These are similar to those listed in the Patient Care Partnership and include the right to:

- be treated with dignity and respect.
- access records of care.
- refuse care.
- maintain privacy and confidentiality.
- have personal items and engage in personal activities and interests.

QUICK REVIEW QUESTION

2. Patients have the right to do all of the following EXCEPT:
   A) refuse care.
   B) choose their nurse.
   C) see their medical record.
   D) expect privacy.

Legal and Ethical Behavior

ETHICS

Ethics are moral principles, values, and duties. Whereas laws are enforceable regulations set by the government, ethics are moral guidelines set and formally or informally enforced by peers, the community, and professional organizations. The following guidelines can help guide the ethical conduct of the nurse aide:

- work within the nurse aide scope of practice
- prioritize the patient's needs over your own
- do not perform any act that will harm the patient
- follow the directions of the nurse
- protect patients' privacy and confidentiality
- report errors immediately

HELPFUL HINT

Nurse aides have an ethical (and sometimes legal) duty to report signs of child or elder abuse.

QUICK REVIEW QUESTION

3. A nurse aide sees a patient steal money from a visitor's purse. The nurse aide should:
   A) alert the nurse that a patient has stolen money.
   B) confront the patient and demand they return the money.
   C) tell the visitor that a patient stole their money.
   D) do nothing and let the visitor address the issue.

LEGAL ISSUES

A **tort** is a wrongful civil act. Tort laws involve the accidental or intentional harm to a person or property that results from the wrongdoing of a person or persons. **Negligence** is a type of tort, defined as failure to offer an acceptable standard of care that is comparable to what a competent health care worker would provide in a similar situation. There are four types of negligence:

- **Nonfeasance**: a willful failure to act when required.
- **Misfeasance**: the incorrect or improper performance of a lawful action.
- **Malfeasance**: a willful and intentional action that causes harm.
- **Malpractice**: a professional's failure to properly execute their duties.

Intentional torts are committed when a person purposefully causes harm to another. Some examples include:

- battery: harmful or offensive contact with another person
- assault: an attempted battery in which there was threat of injury, but no injury occurred
- slander: saying something false about someone that causes damage to their reputation
- libel: writing something false about someone that causes damage to their reputation

Consent for various medical services and health care involves verbal or written permission from the patient. Expressed consent must be **informed**, which requires a trained health care worker explaining the necessary information to the patient so he or she can make an educated decision. **Implied consent** is usually made in life-threatening circumstances and medical emergencies based on the assumption that the patient would consent to lifesaving care. It can also refer to consent suggested by a patient's actions (e.g., extending their arm to have blood drawn).

HELPFUL HINT
Patients have a right to choose or refuse care, and providing care without consent may be considered battery.

QUICK REVIEW QUESTION

4. A patient opening their mouth so the nurse aide can use an oral thermometer is an example of:
   A) informed consent.
   B) implied consent.
   C) battery.
   D) malpractice.

Members of the Health Care Team

NURSE AIDE SCOPE OF PRACTICE

The nurse aide assists the nurse and performs tasks assigned to them by a nurse. The nurse aide may only perform tasks designated to them by appropriate personnel and cannot decide what care a patient needs. The care provided by the nurse aide may include:

- assisting patients with activities of daily living
- collecting patient specimens for testing
- caring for wounds
- assisting with rehabilitation exercises
- any other tasks requested by a nurse for which the nurse aide has been properly trained

The nurse aide should NEVER:

- perform a task they have not been properly trained for
- provide care that has not been requested by a nurse
- alter a patient's care plan

QUICK REVIEW QUESTION

5. Which of the following actions falls within the nurse aide's scope of practice?
   A) obtaining a stool sample
   B) prescribing medications
   C) triaging patients in the waiting room
   D) educating patients at discharge

OTHER MEMBERS OF THE HEALTH CARE TEAM

The nurse aide will work with a variety of health care team members, each of whom performs a specific set of duties. Nurse aides should be familiar with the roles and skills of other health care team members.

certified medical assistant (CMA): A CMA has general administrative office skills and basic nursing skills. They obtain basic medical history and information from patients, take vital signs, collect and test specimens, and assist providers with procedures.

licensed practical nurse (LPN): An LPN is a one-year nurse trained in patient care and licensed by the state.

registered nurse (RN): An RN is a two- or four-year nurse trained in patient care and licensed by the state.

nurse practitioner (NP): An NP is an RN with advanced training to diagnose and treat patients in the health care environment.

clinical nurse specialist (CNS): A CNS has advanced education and training in a specialized field, such as psychiatric care, women's health, or critical care. They can make diagnoses, develop treatment plans, and provide care.

physician assistant (PA): A PA is trained to practice medicine under the supervision of a physician.

physician: Physicians have completed a doctor of medicine (MD) degree. They can diagnose conditions, order procedures, treat patients, and write medication prescriptions for illnesses.

emergency medical technician (EMT): An EMT is trained in the administration of emergency care and transportation of patients to the medical facility.

phlebotomist: Also called an accessioning technician, a phlebotomist is trained in drawing blood and collecting other non-blood specimens for testing.

licensed professional counselor (LPC): LPCs possess a master's or doctoral degree in counseling and will offer collaborative, therapeutic counseling.

licensed clinical social worker (LCSW): LCSWs are licensed to practice in a clinical or counseling setting and directly intermingle with clients to diagnose and treat mental, emotional, and behavioral issues.

occupational therapist registered (OTR): An OTR assists patients as they learn and practice skills for daily living.

physical therapist (PT): The PT assists patients with movement.

QUICK REVIEW QUESTION

6. A phlebotomist is a medical professional who is trained to perform which of the following tasks?
    A) provide hospice care
    B) draw blood
    C) administer medications
    D) perform moderate- and high-complexity laboratory testing

ANSWER KEY

1. **D) is correct.** When questioning a patient through an interpreter, whether the patient cannot hear or does not speak English, the nurse aide should always direct questions to the patient.

2. **B) is correct.** Patients have a right to safe and respectful care, meaning complaints about health care personnel should be addressed promptly. However, the Patient's Bill of Rights does not include the right for patients to choose their nurse.

3. **A) is correct.** The nurse aide has an ethical duty to report the stolen money to their supervisor but should not directly involve themselves in the situation by talking to the patient or visitor.

4. **B) is correct.** When a patient opens their mouth to allow their temperature to be taken, they are giving implied consent.

5. **A) is correct.** Obtaining a stool sample from the patient is within the scope of practice of a nurse aide. The other tasks must be performed by a nurse or physician.

6. **B) is correct.** A phlebotomist is a medical professional trained to draw blood.

SIX: PRACTICE TEST

READ THE QUESTION AND THEN CHOOSE THE CORRECT ANSWER.

1. The nurse aide may use a slide board to:
   (A) reduce risk of injury when transferring clients.
   (B) prevent clients for aspirating while eating.
   (C) prevent injury while the client is bathing.
   (D) assist clients who cannot dress on their own.

2. Contact precautions for a client require a face shield, gown, and gloves. When caring for this client, the nurse aide SHOULD:
   (A) use eyeglasses instead of a face shield.
   (B) remove all PPE after exiting the client's room.
   (C) put on the gloves first, before donning a gown.
   (D) practice hand hygiene after removing all PPE.

3. The administration of nutrients through a catheter inserted into a vein is called:
   (A) NPO.
   (B) parenteral nutrition.
   (C) nasogastric tube feeding.
   (D) IV hydration.

4. To ensure that an accurate blood pressure measurement is taken, the nurse aide SHOULD:
   (A) ask the client to cross their legs at the knee.
   (B) take 2 measurements 30 minutes apart.
   (C) have the client remove tight-fitting clothing.
   (D) use the appropriate size blood pressure cuff.

5. Which of the following findings for an adult client should the nurse aide IMMEDIATELY report to the nurse?
   (A) An axillary temperature of 102.3°F (39°C)
   (B) An oxygen saturation of 96%
   (C) A heart rate of 72 beats per minute
   (D) A weight of 309 pounds

6. Before trimming a client's nails, the toenails should be soaked in warm water for:
   (A) 5 to 10 minutes.
   (B) 10 to 15 minutes.
   (C) 15 to 20 minutes.
   (D) 20 to 25 minutes.

7. A client who is normally responsive does not answer any of the nurse aide's questions when they enter the room to collect vital signs. The nurse aide SHOULD:

    (A) report the change in the client's status to the nurse.
    (B) gently shake the client to see if they are awake.
    (C) tell the client they will be punished if they do not respond to questions.
    (D) come back at a later time to collect vital signs.

8. Which of the following is NOT within the role of the nurse aide when caring for a client on TPN?

    (A) Providing oral hygiene
    (B) Adjusting the rate of infusion
    (C) Applying lip lubricant
    (D) Reporting a client complaint of chest pain to the nurse

9. While shaping a cast, the nurse aide should NOT:

    (A) use pillows to support the cast while it dries.
    (B) use their fingertips to shape the cast.
    (C) report rough cast edges to the nurse.
    (D) elevate a casted arm or leg to reduce swelling.

10. A nurse aide has been asked to dress a client with an IV in a pullover garment. The nurse aide SHOULD:

    (A) disconnect the IV tubing from the bag.
    (B) keep the IV bag below the client.
    (C) put the garment on the client's weak side first.
    (D) tell the nurse that the client cannot be dressed.

11. A client drank 6 oz of coffee. This intake should be recorded as:

    (A) 6 oz.
    (B) 60 mL.
    (C) 30 mL.
    (D) 180 mL.

12. Which of the following is an example of ensuring electrical safety?

    (A) Nailing cords to the floor
    (B) Discarding cords that are damaged or frayed
    (C) Covering table lamps with lampshades
    (D) Turning the lights off when leaving a room

13. While taking vital signs, the nurse aide counts 8 client respirations in 30 seconds. The client's respiratory rate is:

    (A) 4 breaths per minute.
    (B) 8 breaths per minute.
    (C) 16 breaths per minute.
    (D) 32 breaths per minute.

14. Which vitamin promotes the absorption of calcium for healthy bone production?

    (A) Vitamin A
    (B) Vitamin D
    (C) Vitamin E
    (D) Vitamin K

15. Scrambled eggs and shredded meats are on which diet?

    (A) Low sodium
    (B) Clear liquids
    (C) High fiber
    (D) Mechanical soft

16. A client expresses sadness and loneliness about having to be on continuous tube feeds. The nurse aide SHOULD respond:
    (A) "I'm sorry you are having a difficult time with the feedings."
    (B) "We have other clients with feeding tubes. I will see if they want to talk to you."
    (C) "If you get better soon then the tubes can come out."
    (D) "Complaining will only make you feel worse."

17. A nurse aide enters a client's room and finds the client bleeding profusely from an injury on their arm. After putting on gloves, what should the nurse aide do NEXT?
    (A) Direct the client to wash their injury in the sink
    (B) Apply firm, direct pressure to the wound
    (C) Elevate the client's arm above their head
    (D) Remove any objects from the wound

18. When caring for a client who is deaf or hard of hearing, the nurse aide SHOULD:
    (A) describe the layout of the room.
    (B) use a sign language interpreter as needed.
    (C) speak while facing away from the client.
    (D) offer materials in multiple languages.

19. When brushing the teeth of an unconscious client, the nurse aide SHOULD:
    (A) lay the client flat.
    (B) force a toothbrush between the teeth.
    (C) brush the back of the tongue aggressively.
    (D) report any choking symptoms to the nurse.

20. Which method is best for taking a newborn's temperature?
    (A) Tympanic
    (B) Oral
    (C) Rectal
    (D) Axillary

21. When placing a client in a high-Fowler's position, the nurse aide SHOULD:
    (A) raise the foot of the bed above the head of the bed.
    (B) raise the head of the bed to 45 degrees.
    (C) raise the head of the bed to 60 – 90 degrees.
    (D) place the client on their side with the upper leg sharply flexed.

22. When taking a tympanic temperature, the thermometer should be placed:
    (A) under the armpit.
    (B) inside the ear.
    (C) under the tongue.
    (D) in the rectum.

23. When communicating with a client who speaks a different language, the nurse aide SHOULD:
    (A) talk loudly.
    (B) speak quickly.
    (C) use medical terms and abbreviations.
    (D) use gestures and pictures.

24. A stool sample that is black and tarry is called:
    (A) hematuria.
    (B) melena.
    (C) hematemesis.
    (D) hematochezia.

25. When caring for a client who is in rehabilitation after a stroke, the nurse aide SHOULD:
    (A) encourage the client to actively participate in their care.
    (B) perform all activities of daily living for the client.
    (C) ask the client's family to participate in care.
    (D) force the client to learn new skills so they can be independent.

26. Which health care team member tests hearing and prescribes hearing aids?
    (A) Dentist
    (B) Audiologist
    (C) Dietician
    (D) Home health aide

27. A client with a recent above-the-knee amputation of the right leg is reporting pain in their right foot. The client is experiencing what type of pain?
    (A) Acute
    (B) Chronic
    (C) Phantom
    (D) Radiating

28. While caring for a client, the nurse aide notes that the client is sleeping comfortably in bed. The client's heart rate is 87 bpm and regular. Her Foley catheter bag contains 150 mL of pink, cloudy urine. She has consumed 400 mL of water from their water mug. Which finding should the nurse aide report to the nurse IMMEDIATELY?
    (A) Activity level
    (B) Heart rate
    (C) Color and consistency of urine
    (D) Water intake

29. When interviewing a client using an interpreter, the nurse aide SHOULD address questions to the:
    (A) client.
    (B) interpreter.
    (C) nurse.
    (D) client's family.

30. Which of the following instructions should be provided to a client before they provide a stool sample?
    (A) "Do not put toilet tissue into the specimen container."
    (B) "It is okay if urine also collects in the container."
    (C) "Use the specimen container to scoop the stool from the toilet water."
    (D) "Staff will not be able to assist you during voiding."

31. If not visibly soiled or wet, how often, at a minimum, should linens be changed in a long-term care facility?
    (A) Twice daily
    (B) Once daily
    (C) Once per week
    (D) Once per month

32. A nurse aide collected the following amounts from a client's catheter bag:

Time	Output
7:00	210 mL
13:20	365 mL
19:00	295 mL

    The client's total output for this time period should be recorded as:
    (A) 760 mL.
    (B) 790 mL.
    (C) 860 mL.
    (D) 870 mL.

33. Before having the client step on a scale to be weighed, the nurse aide SHOULD:

(A) set the scale to 0.
(B) wash the client's feet.
(C) have the client undress.
(D) weigh another person to calibrate the scale.

34. A client begins to have a seizure. What should the nurse aide do FIRST?

(A) Move furniture and sharp objects away from the client
(B) Leave the client to call 911
(C) Place the client on their back
(D) Put a tongue blade in the client's mouth

35. To brush hair that is matted or tangled, the nurse aide SHOULD:

(A) start brushing at the scalp.
(B) cut out all tangles.
(C) style the hair in a way the aide thinks is best.
(D) begin at the ends of the hair and work toward the scalp.

36. When transferring a client with left-sided weakness from the bed to a wheelchair, the nurse aide SHOULD:

(A) get the client out of bed on their right side.
(B) lift the client from behind.
(C) use a mechanical lift.
(D) position the transfer belt directly under the client's arms.

37. Which client position is the most common for a gynecological or pelvic exam?

(A) Sims
(B) Prone
(C) Fowler's
(D) Lithotomy

38. To promote the client's feeling of safety, the nurse aide SHOULD:

(A) speak sternly with clients who do not follow hospital policies.
(B) use a gentle touch and soft voice while providing care.
(C) always leave the door to the client's room open.
(D) remove dangerous personal objects from the client's room.

39. Which of the following is a violation of the client's right to privacy?

(A) Knocking before entering the room
(B) Keeping the client's body covered with a towel during a bath
(C) Emptying the client's urine drainage bag while visitors are present
(D) Closing the curtain before applying a condom catheter

40. A nurse aide is changing the dressing on a client who had surgery 2 days ago. They notice the edges of the wound have pulled apart and the underlying tissue is exposed. This type of wound should be described as:

(A) eviscerated.
(B) infected.
(C) dehisced.
(D) healed.

41. To avoid the spread of infection while filling a water mug for a client, the nurse aide SHOULD:

(A) avoid letting the ice scoop touch the mug, lid, or straw.
(B) take the water cart into the client's room.
(C) keep the ice chest open when not in use.
(D) leave the lid off the water mug.

42. Sudden onset of weakness on one side of the body and face can be a sign of:
    (A) cardiac arrest.
    (B) a seizure.
    (C) choking.
    (D) a cerebrovascular accident.

43. Which of the following age and pediatric restraint combinations is NOT appropriate to use when collecting vital signs?
    (A) A 1-month-old swaddled with one arm out of the blanket
    (B) A 2-year-old sitting in a chair with the parent in the room
    (C) A 4-year-old sitting back-to-chest in a parent's lap
    (D) A 14-year-old sitting on an exam table with the parent present

44. Standing while bathing increases the client's risk of:
    (A) bladder infections.
    (B) pressure sores.
    (C) falls.
    (D) burns.

45. What is the compression-to-breath ratio for 1-person CPR on an adult?
    (A) 30 compressions to 2 breaths
    (B) 15 compressions to 2 breaths
    (C) 30 compressions to 1 breath
    (D) 15 compressions to 1 breath

46. Accidental urine leakage during exercise or coughing is known as:
    (A) stress incontinence.
    (B) urge incontinence.
    (C) reflex incontinence.
    (D) overflow incontinence.

47. A client is nervous about an upcoming procedure and begins to hyperventilate. How SHOULD the nurse aide attempt to help them?
    (A) Give the client a glass of water
    (B) Tell the client to take deep breaths
    (C) Ask the client to identify the source of their anxiety
    (D) Suggest the client leave the room until they have calmed down

48. When dealing with an angry client, the nurse aide SHOULD:
    (A) be angry and aggressive.
    (B) speak loudly to ensure that they are heard.
    (C) remain calm and use a normal volume and tone of voice.
    (D) be passive, withdrawn, and quiet.

49. Which of the following does NOT typically occur as clients age?
    (A) Appetite increases
    (B) Taste and smell senses dull
    (C) Caloric needs lower
    (D) Digestive juice secretion decreases

50. Which type of waste is NOT matched with its correct disposal container?
    (A) Capillary tubes : sharps container
    (B) Feces : toilet
    (C) Gauze with small amount of blood : regular garbage can
    (D) Linen heavily soiled by blood : dirty linen receptacle

51. A client with alopecia has:
    (A) hair loss.
    (B) an itchy rash.
    (C) excessive sweating.
    (D) body lice.

52. Which of the following is an example of IMPROPER food safety handling?

(A) Washing hands with soap and water before preparing food.

(B) Discarding cooked leftovers from the refrigerator after 4 days.

(C) Using soap to wash all fruits and vegetables.

(D) Keeping cold foods below 40°F (4.5°C)

53. When performing 2-rescuer CPR on an infant, chest compressions should be done using:

(A) the heel of the hand.

(B) the 2-thumb-encircling hands method.

(C) 2 fingers on the sternum.

(D) 2 hands on top of each other with fingers interlocked.

54. If a client weighs 10 kg, what is their weight in pounds?

(A) 4.5 lb

(B) 12.2 lb

(C) 20 lb

(D) 22 lb

55. Pressure ulcers:

(A) are staged according to depth of skin injury.

(B) do not occur over bony prominences.

(C) can occur as early as 8 hours after pressure onset.

(D) only occur in clients over the age of 65.

56. A client shows signs of anaphylaxis while the nurse aide is assisting them with lunch. What should the nurse aide do FIRST?

(A) Induce vomiting

(B) Obtain the client's vital signs

(C) Notify the nurse

(D) Begin rescue breathing and chest compressions

57. Which of the following medical providers CANNOT prescribe medications?

(A) Physician assistant

(B) Nurse practitioner

(C) Physician

(D) Occupational therapist

58. A client with a terminal diagnosis appears tearful and upset. They share with the nurse aide their fears about their diagnosis. Which of the following is the BEST response by the nurse aide?

(A) "I promise the cancer will go away with the radiation treatments."

(B) "I had a friend with the same cancer and she's fine."

(C) "I know how you feel."

(D) "Thank you for sharing your feelings with me. I am sorry you are going through this."

59. A family member wants to visit a client on contact precautions and asks the nurse aide if they need a gown. How SHOULD the nurse aide respond?

(A) "Go on in. The gowns are only for the staff to wear."

(B) "If you will be here for more than 30 minutes, you will need to wear this gown."

(C) "Please wear the gown. It is our policy to protect you, your family, and others."

(D) "You have to wear the gown or security will escort you outside immediately."

60. A client ate 6 of the 8 carrots on their plate. What is their food intake percentage?

(A) 50%

(B) 60%

(C) 66%

(D) 75%

ANSWER KEY

1. **(A)**
   Slide boards are used to protect the safety of clients and nurse aides while transferring clients.

2. **(D)**
   The nurse aide should always wash their hands after removing PPE.

3. **(B)**
   Parenteral nutrition is the administration of nutrients through an IV catheter in a vein instead of the GI tract. It is used when the GI tract cannot be used.

4. **(D)**
   Using the wrong size blood pressure cuff can provide an inaccurate reading.

5. **(A)**
   A fever (a temperature higher than 100.4°F, or 38 °C) should be immediately reported to the nurse.

6. **(C)**
   Toenails should be soaked for 15 to 20 minutes.

7. **(A)**
   Any changes in responsiveness or mental status should be reported to the nurse.

8. **(B)**
   Any adjustments to the rate, placement, or administration of TPN must be done by the nurse. Treat TPN similarly to any IV therapy.

9. **(B)**
   Shape and support a wet cast with palms (NOT fingertips). Fingertips can cause dents in the cast that can lead to pressure sores.

10. **(C)**
    When dressing a client, apply the garment to the weak arm first.

11. **(D)**
    All I&Os should be recorded in milliliters. To convert to metric measurements, multiply by the appropriate conversion factor (in this case, 1 oz = 30 mL).

    $\frac{6 \text{ oz}}{1} \times \frac{30 \text{ mL}}{1 \text{ oz}} = \mathbf{180 \text{ mL}}$

12. **(B)**
    Discarding worn electrical cords is a precaution for ensuring electrical safety.

13. **(C)**
    Respiratory rate is breaths per minute. If the nurse aide counts 8 breaths in 30 seconds, the rate should be recorded as 16 breaths per minute.

14. **(B)**
    Vitamin D promotes the absorption and metabolism of calcium (and phosphorous). It is necessary for healthy bone development.

15. **(D)**
    Soft, semisolid, easily digestible foods such as scrambled eggs and shredded meats are found on a mechanical soft diet.

16. **(A)**
    The nurse aide should listen to the client's concerns and provide emotional support.

17. **(B)**
    The nurse aide should attempt to slow the bleeding by applying pressure to the wound.

18. **(B)**
    Use a sign language interpreter when needed for clients who are deaf or hard of hearing.

19. **(D)**
    Report choking symptoms, signs of pain, bleeding, or coughing to the nurse.

20. **(C)**
    A rectal temperature is taken in infants and children under 3 years old to ensure an accurate measurement.

21. **(C)**
    The head of the bed is raised to between 60 and 90 degrees in high-Fowler's position, 45 in Fowler's, and 30 in semi-Fowler's. Choice D is a description of Sims position.

22. **(B)**
    A tympanic temperature is taken by placing the thermometer in the client's ear.

23. **(D)**
It can be helpful to use gestures and pictures when communicating with clients speaking another language.

24. **(B)**
Melena is black or tarry stool, which results from bleeding in the stomach or upper GI tract. It should be reported to the nurse immediately.

25. **(A)**
The nurse aide's role in client rehabilitation is to promote the client's independence. The nurse aide should encourage the client to participate in their rehabilitation as they are able.

26. **(B)**
An audiologist tests hearing and prescribes hearing aids.

27. **(C)**
Phantom pain is felt in a body part that has been amputated.

28. **(C)**
The pink, cloudy urine should be reported to the nurse immediately. It can be a sign of an infection or other disorder.

29. **(A)**
When using an interpreter, the nurse aide should address the client.

30. **(A)**
Toilet tissue should not be placed into a stool specimen container but instead into a separate trash receptacle or the toilet.

31. **(C)**
Linen should be changed once or twice a week in long-term care or a client's home.

32. **(D)**
Add the three volumes to find the total volume:
210 mL + 365 mL + 295 mL = **870 mL**

33. **(A)**
To take an accurate weight, set the scale to 0 before the client steps on the scale.

34. **(A)**
The client's safety is the most important concern when they are having a seizure. Move furniture and sharp objects away from the client to prevent injury.

35. **(D)**
Begin at the ends of the hair and work toward the scalp to brush tangled or matted hair. This helps ensure client comfort.

36. **(A)**
Get the client out of bed on their strong side and use the strong side first for transferring.

37. **(D)**
In a lithotomy position, the client is on their back with their feet in stirrups. This is a common position for a pelvic exam or vaginal birth.

38. **(B)**
Using a gentle touch and speaking in a soft voice are techniques that promote the client's feelings of safety.

39. **(C)**
Emptying the client's urine bag before visitors arrive respects the client's right to privacy.

40. **(C)**
Dehiscence occurs when the wound layers pull apart or separate. Clients may say they felt the wound "pop" open.

41. **(A)**
Avoid letting the ice scoop touch the mug, lid, or straw to prevent the spread of microbes between the water mug and ice scoop.

42. **(D)**
A cerebrovascular accident, or stroke, can cause weakness to one side of the body and face.

43. **(B)**
For comfort and safety, toddlers should be positioned in a parent's lap in a bear hug or back-to-chest position.

44. **(C)**
Standing while bathing can increase the risk of falls and dizziness.

45. **(A)**

One-person CPR on an adult or a child uses 30 compressions followed by 2 breaths.

46. **(A)**

Stress incontinence is loss of urine during exercise or certain straining movements such as sneezing, laughing, or coughing.

47. **(B)**

The nurse aide can assist the client in changing their physiologic response by directing them to take deep breaths. This will help the client focus on the present moment and help to alleviate the panic.

48. **(C)**

When dealing with an angry client, the nurse aide should remain calm and use a moderate volume and tone of voice.

49. **(A)**

Appetite decreases in older clients.

50. **(D)**

Linen that is lightly soiled can go in the dirty linen receptacle. However, linen that is heavily soiled by blood should be placed in a biohazard bag.

51. **(A)**

Alopecia is a condition that causes excessive hair loss.

52. **(C)**

Do not use soap or detergent to wash fruits and vegetables; they should be rinsed with tap water.

53. **(B)**

During 2-rescuer CPR on an infant, the 2-thumb-encircling hands method should be used.

54. **(D)**

Multiply the weight in pounds by the appropriate conversion factor (1 kg = 2.2 lb).

$$\frac{10 \text{ kg}}{1} \times \frac{2.2 \text{ lb}}{1 \text{ kg}} = \textbf{22 lb}$$

55. **(A)**

Pressure ulcers are staged according to depth of skin injury. They can occur as early as 2 – 6 hours after onset of pressure. Major causes are pressure, friction, and shearing that cause skin breakdown. These ulcers can occur in clients of any age, not just those over 65.

56. **(C)**

The priority for the nurse aide is to notify the nurse.

57. **(D)**

Occupational therapists cannot prescribe medications.

58. **(D)**

The best response when talking with upset clients is to acknowledge their pain and their feelings, show gratitude for their openness, and offer support.

59. **(C)**

Politely tell visitors to wear the proper PPE to protect themselves, the client, and their family.

60. **(D)**

Divide the amount of food eaten by the original amount:

$$\frac{6}{8} = 0.75$$

Multiple by 100 to convert to a percent:

0.75 x 100 = **75%**

Follow the link below to take your second CNA practice test and to access other online study resources:

https://www.ascenciatestprep.com/cna-online-resources

www.ingramcontent.com/pod-product-compliance
Lightning Source LLC
Chambersburg PA
CBHW080846020526
44114CB00045B/2678